Primary and Secondary Education in Sierra Leone: An Evaluation of >50 years of Policies and Practices

Ebenezer 'Solo' Collier

Sierra Leonean Writers Series

**Primary and Secondary Education in Sierra Leone:
An Evaluation of >50years of Policies and Practices**
Copyright © 2012 by Ebenezer 'Solo' Collier
All rights reserved.

No part of this book may be reproduced in any form or by any electronic or mechanical means except by reviewers for the public press without written permission from the publishers.

ISBN: 978-99910-54-53-7

This Edition: March 2016

Sierra Leonean Writers Series
Warima/Freetown/Accra
120 Kissy Road, Freetown, Sierra Leone
Publisher: Prof. Osman Sankoh (Mallam O.) publisher@sl-writers-series.org

Primary and Secondary Education in Sierra Leone

DEDICATION

To the memory of my mother,

Olive Vivat Collier, nicknamed 'Lorloh'

To my wife, Avril,

for her love and encouragement.

ACKNOWLEDGEMENTS

Special thanks to the former Minister of Education, Dr. Alpha Wurie who provided me with transportation and contacts to the participants throughout the country between 2007 and 2010 in my collection of data and interviews. I am also grateful to all the officials of the Ministry of Education, the West Africa Examination Council, and the Central Statistics Office who provided me with the data I needed to do my research for this book.

I extend my sincere appreciation to the principals and teachers who devoted their time and opened their minds to my interviews. Their contributions to the success of this research will forever be remembered and cherished. I acknowledge with sincere gratitude the professionalism and excellent editing of the manuscript by Dr. Mohamed Kamanda. To all my friends, especially the 'Cyclades' group whose encouragement during the course of writing this book motivated my desire for success.

I have been deeply touched by the unyielding support and encouragement of my relatives, especially my wife and brothers. I am indeed thankful to the almighty God for providing all the human and material support for me to accomplish this goal.

PREFACE

Chapter one describes the evolution and orientation of educational administration and policies in Sierra Leone, and develops the theme for the literature review in chapter two on pre-colonial/traditional-indigenous education through colonial education and post-independence education. In chapter three, attempt is made to examine the trends in educational policies during colonial, post-colonial, and post-civil war eras, and the backgrounds to the trends which existed during those periods on student enrollment, teachers, and students' performances/ achievement during the past 50 years. In chapter four, statistical data are used to show how and to what extent educational policies influence the educational practices and standards at the primary and secondary school levels. Chapter five presents the responses of interviews conducted with school administrators, primary and secondary school teachers of their perceptions on the needs to improve education in Sierra Leone. Chapter six analyses the effects of the educational policies on primary and secondary education by qualifying the quantitative data given in chapter four. In the final chapter, information is given about the challenges of the educational system, and how it can assist educational leaders in Sierra Leone develop effective educational models.

Ebenezer 'Solo' Collier

FOREWORD

Colonial education was instituted in Sierra Leone as a consequence of the activities of British philanthropic and missionary bodies from the late 19th to mid 20th century. It was largely in the hands of Christian missionaries introduced in the form of evangelism and as part of Western missionary enterprise. Such education basically ignored the achievements and contributions of the indigenous populations and for the most part, did not cultivate the African student's self esteem and pride.

Freetown became the centre for secondary school education, not only for those Sierra Leoneans of influence, connection or wealth but also as a centre for secondary education for other British West Africans from Ghana, Nigeria and the Gambia. It was not until a protectorate was declared in the hinterland that the colonial government took charge of education as a tool for economic exploitation as well as containing local resistance to white rule. As a direct consequence of the Hut- Tax War of 1898, a boy's school was created in 1906 in Bo, for sons and nominees of chiefs.

The policy of entrance by genealogy was vital for reducing ethnic tensions by administering boys of various ethnic backgrounds together. This however fostered elitism and affected access to school. It took another fifty years for the first 'Open' school which catered for non sons and nominees of chiefs to be opened in 1953, quickly followed by Government sponsored secondary schools in Magburaka, Kenema, Jimmy and some other faith based mission schools. Thus at independence, with a population of about 2.1 million, access to secondary education was still very low. The idea of rapid expansion caught on very quickly as reflected in the phenomenal increase in primary and secondary education. This was largely driven by granting recognition to the new schools that were established, by

Primary and Secondary Education in Sierra Leone

payment of salaries of qualified teachers along with covering operating and development costs.

Following the attainment of self–determination, policy makers in many African countries expressed disillusionment with the imported western models of schooling and sought to adopt alternate approaches that were designed to promote aspects of education that were of relevance to them. Sierra Leone's educational development was guided by several comprehensive educational policies and program. Series of educational reforms were undertaken intended to make education compatible with the social needs of the people. Policies were then formulated to overhaul the system and make it accessible to all irrespective of status taking cues from global conferences such as the Development of Education in Africa sponsored by UNESCO in 1961, which subsequently gave birth to the 'Education for All' movement that supported changes to education in Sierra Leone. The establishment of the National Commission for Basic Education in 1993, the 1995 New Education Policy for Sierra Leone and the Education Master Plan in 1997 all have links to the 'Education for All' approach.

The civil war in 1991-2002 had overtones of anger of young people resulting in adverse effect on the education sector: destruction of school infrastructure, displacement of teachers, disorientation and psychological trauma among children and weakened institutional capacity to manage the system. The reconstruction of hundreds of schools across the country and training and provision of attractive incentives for teachers occasioned the recovery of the education sector. There were substantial legal reforms culminating in the enactment of two Acts between 2001and 2004 namely: Education Act 2004 which replaced the Education Act of 1964, outlining the structure of the educational system, management and control of various actors including local authorities; the Local Government Act which saw the transfer of the management and supervision of basic education from central to local governments, following the revival of local councils and marking decentralisation of education after 30 years of centralised governance.

Free tuition fees at the primary level and the abolishment of examination fees at the end of primary, Junior Secondary and Senior Secondary Schools sectors i.e (NPSE, BECE and WASSCE) have strengthened both access and school retention whilst provision of school materials have improved quality. There has been movement from a predominantly grammar school type of education during colonial /post independence periods to a grammar school/vocational/ technical education in post civil war era. As we strengthen the management of 'Extractive Minerals' it is hoped that free compulsory primary and secondary education will be with us sooner; rather than later.

This book authored by Dr. Ebenezer 'Solo' Collier, gives details of policies, programmes and statistical outcomes. It is important, particularly for policy makers, as it may serve as input to the debate on future education policy development and has the potential for contributing to research literature on implementation of educational policies. Sierra Leoneans should access relevant knowledge of the development of education during the 50 years of Independence which has been lacking and which this book presents. As such, it can also be a useful reference material for college and university lecturers.

Dr. Alpha Wurie
Associate Professor of Chemistry, Fourah Bay College,
University of Sierra Leone
Proprietor, RAMSY Laboratory
Former Minister of Education (1996-2007)
Sierra Leone Government

ABBREVIATIONS

BECE: Basic Education Certificate Examination
CREPS: Complementary Rapid Education for Primary Schools
EFA: Education for All
GCE: General Certificate Examination
IDA: International Development Assistance
NPSE: National Primary School Examination
SLIHS: Sierra Leone Integrated Household Survey
UPE: Universal Primary Education
UNESCO: United Nations Educational, Scientific and Cultural Organization
WAEC: West African Examinations Council
WASSCE: West Africa Senior School Certificate Examination

Table of Contents

Dedication	i
Acknowledgements	ii
Preface	iii
Foreword	iv
Abbreviations	vii
List of Tables	ix
List of Figures	x
CHAPTER 1: Introduction	1
1.0 Background	3
1.1 Orientation of Educational Policies	10
CHAPTER: Literature Review	17
2.0 Pre-colonial/Traditional-Indigenous Education	17
2.1 Colonial Education	20
2.2 Post-Independence Education	29
CHAPTER 3: Trends in Educational Policies	38
3.0 Colonial	39
3.1 Post-Colonial/Independence	41
3.2 Post-Civil War	42
CHAPTER 4: Trends in Educational Practices	46
4.0 Student Enrollment	46
4.1 Teachers	50
4.2 Student Performance/Achievement	52
CHAPTER 5: Current Perceptions	62
CHAPTER 6: Analysis	73
6.0 School Enrollment	74
6.1 Academic Achievements	75
6.2 Resources	77
6.3 Teachers	77
6.4 Decentralization	79
CHAPTER 7: Planning for the future in Education	84
REFERENCES	93

LIST OF TABLES

Table 4.1	Primary Schools Enrollment	46
Table 4.2	Secondary Schools Enrollment	46
Table 4.3	Percentage of Qualified Teachers	50
Table 4.4	Common Entrance/National Primary Schools Exams Pass Rates	54
Table 4.5	Basic Education Certificate Exams Pass Rates	55
Table 4.6	WAEC/GCE-O Level/WASSCE Pass Rates	56
Table 4.7	Primary Schools Demography by Regions (2009/10)	57
Table 4.8	Secondary Schools Demography by Regions (2009/10)	57
Table 4.9	National Primary Schools Exams Pass Rates by Regions (2009/10)	59
Table 4.10	Basic Education Certificate Exams Pass Rates by Regions (2009/10)	60
Table 4.11	WASSCE Pass Rates by Region (2009/10)	60
Table 5.1	Primary School Administrator's Perception	62
Table 5.2	Secondary School Administrator's Perception	63
Table 5.3	Primary Schools Administrators' Perception by Region	65
Table 5.4	Secondary Schools Administrators' Perception by Region	66
Table 5.5	Primary School Teacher's Perception	67
Table 5.6	Secondary School Teacher's Perception	68
Table 5.7	Primary Schools Teachers' Perception by Region	69
Table 5.8	Secondary Schools Teachers' Perception by Region	70

LIST OF FIGURES

Figure 4.1	Student Enrollments –Primary Schools	47
Figure 4.2	Student Enrollments –Secondary Schools	47
Figure 4.3	Percentage of School-Age Children in Schools	48
Figure 4.4	Percentage of Qualified Teachers in Schools	51
Figure 4.5	Pass Rates of School Exit Exams	56
Figure 4.6	Primary Schools Enrollments by Regions (2009/10)	58
Figure 4.7	Secondary Schools Enrollments by Regions (2009/10)	58
Figure 4.8	Percentage of Qualified Teachers by Regions (2009/10)	59
Figure 4.9	School Exit Exams Pass Rates by Regions (2009/10)	60

CHAPTER 1

Introduction

Sierra Leone, a small country on the west coast of Africa, has an area of approximately 28,000 square miles. It is bounded on the north-west and north-east by the Republic of Guinea, on the southeast by the Republic of Liberia and on the south-west by the Atlantic Ocean. Sierra Leone lies between latitudes 7 and 10 degrees north and longitudes 10 and 13 degrees west. In 2006 the population was estimated to be five million (Central Statistics, 2006)) comprising 15 ethnic groups: Mende, Temne, Creole, Limba, Loko, Fulla, Madingo, Susu, Yalunka, Koranko, Sherbro, Kono, Kru, Kissi, and Krim, all co-existing in a diverse landscape rich in gold, bauxite, iron ore, diamonds, and rutile. Sierra Leone has a vast expanse of fertile agricultural land producing rice for staple and coffee, cocoa, ginger, groundnut for export, as well as an abundant amount of off-shore fishing. It is also in the process of developing what is estimated to be one of the world's largest deposits of iron ore, while offshore oil reserves discovered in 2009 are currently being explored for commercial viability.

This book compares the effects of educational policies on primary and secondary education in Sierra Leone during colonial, post-independence, and post-civil war eras. It examines trends in observable and measurable changes and developments in educational policies from the colonial period to present. It also assesses how these policies influenced the educational practices and standards, such as student enrolment, teacher qualification, student-teacher ratio, drop-out rate and academic achievements at the primary and secondary levels of schooling. In addition, it examines the perception of educational policy makers, leaders, and teachers on the current needs to improve education in Sierra Leone.

The following questions were used to examine the trends in the educational policies from pre-colonial times to present.
1. What were the trends in educational policies during the colonial period?
2. What were the trends in educational policies during the post-colonial / independence period?
3. What are the trends in educational policies in the post-civil war era?
4. What were the backgrounds to the trends which existed in those periods?
5. How and to what extent did these policies influence the educational practices and standards at the primary and secondary school levels?
6. How did these policies impact the human resource needs of Sierra Leone?
7. What, in the perception of current educational policy makers, leaders, teachers and community advocates, are current needs for improving education in Sierra Leone?

This chapter describes the evolution and orientation of educational administration and policies in Sierra Leone, and develops the theme for the literature review in chapter two on pre-colonial/traditional-indigenous education through colonial education and post-independence education. In chapter three, attempt is made to examine the trends in educational policies during colonial, post-colonial, and post-civil war eras, and the backgrounds to the trends which existed during those periods on student enrollment, teachers, and students' performances /achievement during the past 50 years. In chapter four, statistical data are used to show how and to what extent educational policies influence the educational practices and standards at the primary and secondary school levels. Chapter five presents the responses of interviews conducted with school administrators, primary and secondary school teachers of their perceptions on the needs to improve education in Sierra Leone. Chapter six analyses the effects of the educational policies on primary and secondary education by discussing the quantitative data given in chapter four. The final chapter provides information on the challenges of the current education system and sheds light on possible ways in which educational leaders in Sierra Leone could develop effective educational models.

1.0 Background

There are 4,928 primary schools with about 1.4 million students, consisting of 79% of school age children. 70% of these school age children are males and 69% are females. 134,000 students attend 282 secondary schools constituting 40% of secondary school age children. 72% of these children are males and 59% are females (Population Census, 2006).

European contacts with Sierra Leone were among the earliest in West Africa. Some of the main factors for these contacts were the geography of the country, philanthropy and colonization. Early Sierra Leone history is very unclear, but what is known is that most of the arrivals in Sierra Leone were around the 1400's.

During the late 18th and early 19th centuries, there were two distinct groups of inhabitants. The first (and much smaller) group comprised the descendants or the liberated slaves. Following the abolition of slavery in England in 1772, it was decided that the slaves who had thus regained freedom should be resettled in a territory in Africa, and Sierra Leone was chosen as a suitable site. Over 300 freed slaves arrived in Sierra Leone in 1787 (Fafunwa, 1963). Others followed later and soon a settlement grew up in what was aptly named 'Free-Town'. The liberated slaves often referred to as 'Creoles', were allocated plots of land for cultivation in Freetown and were also provided with food and clothing. Later on, they spread to the outlying villages, most of which were given typically European names such as Bathurst, Regent, Waterloo and Hastings. The whole area later became known as the 'colony' of Sierra Leone.

The other and much larger group comprised the original inhabitants of Sierra Leone who had lived in the country for many years, even before the arrival of any European. These original inhabitants belonged to various ethnic groups. They lived within their own ethnic regions and were able to preserve their customs and cultural heritage.

Before the colonial era, education was suited for the conditions of traditional life. Social customs, religious beliefs, cultural norms and civic duties were taught to instill the required obligations and responsibilities to the communities. The skills acquired were intended to enable the initiates to efficiently perform such duties as building homes, caring for the family, rearing domestic animals, producing crops, fishing and hunting. Further, the technical skills of making implements and weapons, coupled with special competencies in such trades as blacksmithing and medicine, were usually passed from father to son by life apprenticeship.

Colonial education was instituted in Sierra Leone as a consequence of the activity of British philanthropic and missionary bodies and lasted from the late 19th century to the mid 20th century. However, during the colonial period, with the introduction of new methods in educational administration, organization and curriculum content, the purpose of education became unclear due largely to the conflict between the colonial idea of educational structure and method on the one hand, and the traditional-indigenous approach on the other. British control in Sierra Leone did not extend into the hinterland of the country until the closing years of the nineteenth century when a Protectorate was declared in 1896. Thereafter formal education, which had been left largely to Christian mission societies, was taken over by the colonial civil government and used as "a systematic and measurable tool for economic exploitation, reduction of local resistance to white rule, transformation of indigenous outlooks, and meeting the limited needs of the colonial civil service" (Kanu, 2007, p.2). Wilson (1963) observed

Primary and Secondary Education in Sierra Leone

that there was a sharp conflict between the incoming education of the West and the traditional system of education.

In the late colonial and post-colonial period, educational development in Sierra Leone had been characterized by three main processes: (a) a massive explosion at all levels, (b) the provision for technical and professional instruction, and (c) the Africanization of the curricula. Datta (1984) noted that in the struggle for power, the African elite realized the importance of drawing the masses to their side against the colonial masters. In the ensuing process, they soon discovered the relevance of education as an agency for effective communication with the masses as well as mobilizing them. Education was also seen as a means of bringing about economic development and cultural self-assertion. Further to this instrumental value, there was a general recognition that education was something 'good' in itself. As a result demand for mass education grew.

The evolution of the educational administration began in the early twentieth century when the Department of Education was established as an advisory body to the governor. A Director of Education was appointed to head the Department of Education, and work in collaboration with the Education Committee (Sumner, 1966). In 1924, the Education Ordinance instituted the Board of Education which replaced the Education Committee. In 1952, the Ministry of Education was established to work jointly with the Department of Education. Furthermore, the Education Ordinance of 1953 clarified the relationship between: (a) Ministry of Education and the Department of Education; and (b) Ministry of Education and the Director of Education (Ministry of Education of Sierra Leone, 1966). Eight years later in 1961, the Department of Education and its head, the Director of Education, were absorbed into the Ministry of Education and the Minister was charged with the responsibility for educational planning. Directly responsible to the Minister of Education were two principal officials: the Permanent Secretary and the Chief Education officer, the latter was formerly called Director of

Education. These two positions have now been combined as Director General of Education. The Permanent Secretary was responsible for monitoring the operation of the secretary and was also concerned with financial matters, such as the award of scholarships to students who pursued studies both in Sierra Leone and overseas. The Chief Education Officer, on the other hand, served as the Minister's leading advisor on professional matters. The Chief Education Officer acted in the additional capacities of chairman of the Board of Education and head of all Education Officers. The Board of Education, whose representation embraced the University of Sierra Leone, the Provincial Councils, the Western and Rural area Councils, the Amalgamated Teachers' Union, the Moslem, Roman Catholic and the United Christian Council Missions, also acted as advisory body to the Ministry of Education. In addition, power was vested in the Minister to appoint advisory committees for specific assignments in such professional matters as production and evaluation of textbooks and revision of the syllabus. Directly responsible to the Chief Education Officer were the Principal Education Officer of Teacher Education, the Principal Education Officer of Primary Education, the Principal Education Officer of Secondary Education and the Principal Education Officer Technical and Vocational Education.

In 1956, the UNESCO Expert, W.A.B. Goodwin, recommended the introduction of a cadre of school inspectors and supervisors charged with the responsibility of constant review of curricula needs with the teachers (Sierra Leone Government, 1970). The inspectors were officers of the central government, placed in the position of implementing the educational policy of the Ministry of Education. Prior to 1956, inspectors were constituted as a separate body of the mission organization or as individuals appointed by the government on the basis of their professional experience and good reputation.

There were two categories of inspectors: (a) a set for primary schools appointed in 1956 (b) a set for the secondary schools appointed in 1970 (Sierra Leone Government, 1970). In 1970 there were 13 inspectors for the primary schools and 13 supervisors, in addition to four senior inspectors stationed in the four political regions of the country. Each of the 12 provincial districts had one inspector and a supervisor, and each of the three provinces had a senior inspector. While the senior inspectors were stationed at provincial headquarters, the inspectors were based at the district administrative towns. The western area had two inspectors, one of whom was a senior inspector. By this arrangement the supervisors worked under the inspectors, who in turn played a subordinate role to the senior inspectors. All of the officers worked as a team under the Chief Education Officer.

The importance of educational expansion was re-emphasized by the All Africa States Conference held in Addis Ababa in 1967. The Conference also acknowledged the importance of primary education and African countries resolved to provide: (a) free universal primary education by 1980; (b) secondary education to at least 30% of those students who had successfully completed primary education; (c) higher education to at least 20% of those candidates who had successfully completed secondary education, and (d) to aim at improving the quality of education at all levels of the education system.

At the recommendation of the Addis Ababa Conference, a number of auxiliary services were set up at the Ministry of Education. For example, the post of Principal Education Officer for planning with the assistance of a statistician was created and filled in the early 1970's. The main task of the Education Planning Officer was to prepare detailed descriptions of the existing educational system in six categories: primary, secondary, teacher education, vocational and technical education, higher education, and adult education. The description was to include not only the number of schools, their geographical distribution, and enrollment in relation to school-age population of the geographic unit, but also such quality criteria as the range of grades offered, holding power of the schools and the adequacy of equipment available to the teacher. The teaching aids branch of the Ministry of Education was also established. It consisted of: (a) the publication unit, (b) the school broadcasting unit and (c) the audiovisual centre, each of which was supervised by an education officer (Sierra Leone Government, 1970).

Since Independence, Sierra Leone's educational development was guided by several comprehensive educational policies and programs. Most of them had the official approval of government, although the others which did not still impacted on policy and planning. The most important official policy statements were the White Paper on Educational Development of 1958; the Report of Education Planning Group of 1961; the Ten Year Plan of Economic and Social Development 1962/63 - 1971/72; the Development Program in Education 1964-70; the White Paper on Educational Policy of 1970 and 1995; and the Education Act of 2004.

Policy makers and professional educators in Sierra Leone are currently confronted with many difficult problems which include providing students with relevant job-entry skills, designing instruction for career development, responding to the complex needs of less privileged students, and keeping pace with social, economic, and technological developments. With the legacies of a colonial power and its social, cultural and political influences, the trend of education in Sierra Leone had followed a pattern of growth and establishment of an elite subculture with strong western influence. Though significant strides have been made in restructuring educational policies and practices, developments and improvements, education has been disproportionately quantitative rather than qualitative: increase in student enrollment had not met with increase in student achievement/ performance.

The current plea for the adaptation of education to the African cultural setting is not new. As early as 1920, the Phelps-Stokes Commission Report influenced the Advisory Committee

Primary and Secondary Education in Sierra Leone

to facilitate the introduction of a number of British educational policies in the tropical African colonies. Basically, the aims of education for Africa, as implied in the Phelps-Stokes Commission recommendations and endorsed by the Advisory Committee, were to foster: (a) preservation and transmission of the cultural heritage of the past, (b) ability to cope with the existing problems and (c) a sense of preparation for the future.

Before the introduction of western formal education, the African societies in general, and that of Sierra Leone in particular, had practiced an indigenous education system. The indigenous system was channeled through three main educational agencies, namely: (a) Intimate personal relationship within the family which were undeniably the most fundamental (b) an informal education system conducted on the basis of contact with peers and the communities at large and (c) organized traditional institutions set aside for the introduction of youth in recognition of their age at the puberty stage of growth and development. Lebby (1980) described the education process monitored in these manners as couched on a wide range of philosophical foundations including communal, preparational, perennial, and wholistic. He noted that "it was communal because it was egalitarian; preparational because of its pre-occupational orientation, perennial because of its life-long education thrust, and wholistic because of its advocacy for mastery level achievement toward which the learner was guided" (p. 173).

Colonial education was not in fact deliberate but was introduced in the form of evangelism and as part of Western missionary enterprise (Ayandele, 1971). The government undertook a series of educational reform movements. These reforms were intended to be compatible with social needs, as well as such contemporary issues as global interdependence, knowledge explosion, rural-urban drift, population increase, and nationwide unemployment with its attendant social problems.

In the period after 1970, the socio-economic situation in the country got progressively worse, adversely affecting the education sector in particular. The formal system of education then constituted primary schooling from the age of five, followed by secondary education leading to Sixth Form and Advanced Levels, culminating (for the few) in university education. The system was elitist and highly biased towards the top twenty five percentile in academic intelligence. The emphasis was on liberal education leading to the central and conservative professions of law, medicine and teaching.

In 1991, a rebel movement emerged under the banner of the Revolutionary United Fund (RUF). The rebels captured up to 80% of the countryside and later occupied the capital of Freetown. In addition to a substantial portion of the population being displaced in refugee camps, the impact of the war on schooling in Sierra Leone was devastating. Thousands of children were killed, raped or mutilated. A large number of teachers were forced to flee the country and a substantial proportion of the schools were either totally destroyed or badly damaged (Sierra Leone Ministry of Youth, Education and Sports, 2001).

1.1 Orientation of Educational Policies

Every society, whether simple or complex, has its own system of educating its young ones. The education for the 'good life' is one of the most persistent concerns throughout the ages. The progressive schools are concerned more with the individual child's interests and needs. Phenix (1961) identified three causes why people find it difficult to understand what is really 'good': (a) ignorance (b) the boundless depth and richness of reality and (c) self-centeredness.

The goal of education and the method of approach may differ from place to place, nation to nation, but the need for goals in individual and social life sets a clear and exacting task for education. There may be a number of different educational policies and practices, which similarly reflect different valuations and orientations of the educational community.

Education is inherently a controversial field of theory and

practical action, for it is concerned both with fundamental human rights and the nurturing of personality and also with social change and the ideals at which it should aim. It is a worthwhile activity, concerned with the values a society considers important for its citizens and with objectives and outcomes that will enhance the quality of the society, as well as improve the lives of its inhabitants. As Phenix (1961) puts it, "an 'educated' person whose information and ability are directed to no personally appropriated worthy *ends* is a menace to himself and to society" (p. 11). Education poses essentially the same problems in all societies, but the solutions adopted for them as embodied in the respective educational systems differ from one society to another and are dependent upon the nature of the individual society and its goals.

Since the attainment of self-government, policy makers in many African countries have expressed disillusionment with imported western models of schooling and sought to adopt alternative approaches designed to promote rural development, particularly the integration of agricultural, vocational and technical training into general primary, secondary, and teacher education programs (Nyerere, as cited in Resnick, 1968). School-leaver dissatisfaction to access the work force has led to the persistent questioning of the relevance of the school curriculum and has forced policy makers to believe that the frustration of young people will be overcome and ensure their willingness to participate in the life and work of their communities by providing more relevant programs (Fafunwa, 1982).

Few scholars today would deny that colonial education in Africa was Eurocentric and culturally/socially irrelevant. Colonial education ignored the achievements and contributions of the indigenous populations and their ancestries. For the most part, it did not cultivate the African student's self-esteem and pride. Kallon (1996) argued that colonial education has continued not only to be irrelevant, but also alienate the learner from reality. The system has been accused of failing to serve the needs of the people and instead, perpetuated white, ethnic and patriarchal hegemonies and class biases.

In the early fifties, Sierra Leone joined the West African Examinations Council (WAEC) together with the other three former British colonies: Nigeria, Ghana and Gambia. They developed their own syllabi and gradually removed themselves from the umbilical cord of the Cambridge School Examination syndicate. The most important subjects to benefit from this change were social sciences, geography and history. The students began to make Africa, and not Europe, their center of interest, and started to learn for the first time, about their own past.

In Sierra Leone, education is an amalgam of the traditional-indigenous system and the formal system of western education. These two systems of education interact in an informal sort of way to their mutual benefit or detriment. Equally, the educational policies are formulated and prescribed by a centralized bureaucracy – the Ministry of Education – where the repercussions of policies invariably assume national significance. Illiteracy continues to be a major drawback to accelerated and balanced national development. The illiteracy crisis has continued to be a nightmare and attempts to reverse the situation through education so as to aid and ensure sustainable national development have been futile, due to many insurmountable obstacles. The dropout phenomenon has been an endemic problem among students and has continued to create disparities between the rural and the urban sectors. Recent statistics show that educational facilities and accompanying job opportunities continue to remain inadequate in the cities and towns; the rural communities fair even worse. This persistent neglect has triggered rural-urban migration, with people trooping into towns in search of jobs to escape from a life of deprivation fraught with illiteracy and ignorance, disease, malnutrition and poverty.

The general orientation of educational policies in Sierra Leone demonstrates the necessity for the re-organization of the system. There is persistent popular demand for more education.

Primary and Secondary Education in Sierra Leone

There are mainly three different aspects of this problem, relating respectively to obsolescence, irrelevance and inappropriateness. With knowledge, technology and job characteristics all changing very rapidly, there is today the problem of keeping the content of education up to date, of giving students an education that will equip them for the different world they will live tomorrow. The question of relevance has generally been raised with regard to all levels of the education system, but with a stronger focus on the primary and secondary levels that provide schooling opportunities to a greater majority of the populace.

In spite of the many efforts made to achieve balance and progress in popular education during the colonial period, there was always disparity between the stated goals and plans of education, and what was actually achieved in the field. Education was not, for the most part a systematic program; rather it was as varied as the missionary bodies that were largely responsible for it. The underlying reasons for this as Makulu (1971) points out, were that "educational planning had little relation to the African conditions and African life; that although education has ceased to be regarded as a philanthropic service, it was still considered as a means to an end: the production of junior civil servants and, in the case of missions, the strengthening of church membership" (p.91). Alternatively, education was considered as just one more of the public social services and not as an important process of human and social development. In this way, the colonial system of education "emphasized and encouraged the individualistic instincts of mankind, instead of his co-operation instincts. It led to the possession of individualistic material wealth being the major criterion of social merit and worth" (Nyerere, as cited in Resnick, 1968, p. 51).

Nicol (1991) indicated that a good number of documents and studies revealed that politicians and educational planners have demonstrated a proclivity for interpreting educational growth in terms of infrastructural growth or expansion. Perhaps the dominant motivation in the current trend of policy-making in Sierra Leone is the tendency to view education as being centrally responsible for economic development. The general assumption seems to be that given the right curriculum that is skill oriented, it will produce the needed manpower to promote socio-economic development.

There were many formulations in government plans for the development of education, usually couched in idealistic, rather than practical terms and often expressing hopes such as the following:

1. That better education could overcome ignorance and open the way for individuals to lead richer lives, to establish better social relationships within communities, and so enable the local communities to gain in self-respect and become more democratic and responsible, more able to take initiatives for their own improvement and to become more outward looking.
2. That to improve education could contribute to economic growth, thus raising the general standard of living and helping towards better employment opportunities, health, housing, etc.
3. That education could improve the quality of rural life, especially the level of agricultural skills with the aid of literacy and the opportunities for a richer cultural life.
4. That it could improve the training in skills for the development of industries, and also modern social services, increasing the readiness to learn new techniques required for innovation and change.
5. That it could be the most effective means of developing a more equitable society, with better opportunities for individuals in the countryside as well as in towns, with less extremes of poverty and affluence, more responsible leaders and administrators.
6. That education could contribute to nation-building, by fostering a growing respect for each nation's own culture and traditions and by aiding the development of political maturity, which would be capable of combining orderly

leadership of thought and expression and respect for individual rights.

Such statements reflect the idealism of the first post-independence phase, before financial limitations had begun to bite and before there had been time to think critically about some of the underlying educational problems. One of the key problems facing Sierra Leone's education today is to integrate the educational system into the type of society it serves. Even though in recent years, there have been a marked increase in student enrolment at all levels of the educational ladder, the patterns of departmental and subject structure, educational type, and the relative expenditures by levels have not markedly changed from what prevailed over the last four decades. The school system can be criticized for its failure to achieve many of its goals and for the harmful nature of much of its impact upon the society.

'Education for all', as it was envisioned by the member states of the Addis Ababa Conference, remained an unattainable goal for Sierra Leone. Education for Sierra Leone or any developing nation can no longer be seen as a value per se for the advancement of the elites, but it has to play a supportive role in the advancement and multi-sided development of the masses in Third World countries (Nyerere, as cited in Resnick, 1968). The less intellectually able or those with practical gifts and abilities were labeled as failures. No serious attempts were made to cater for the wide range of abilities, interests and aptitudes. Education did not come to grips with the special problems of a developing country or of a poor nation pulled apart by different languages, tribal affiliations and cultures.

As education is generally regarded as the key to national development, proposals for nation building have included the reform of inherited educational systems which were established to maintain the colonial social order and which continue to function to foster neo-colonial dependency, promote elitism, and inadequately prepare individuals for living successfully in their communities and in a rapidly changing world (Kanu, 2007). The system succeeded admirably in producing excellent scholars, who were successful clones of the western world; but it woefully failed to nurture proud, creative, efficient and self-assured Sierra Leoneans.

CHAPTER 2

Literature Review

The history of African education can be divided into three main periods. The first can be described as the period of the coming-of-age ceremonies which provided the principal education for the African child. This period can be referred to as the African indigenous education system. The second period, dominated by the Christian missionary activities, was characterized by the evangelization of the African through education as the potent instrument. The third period, which began after independence, witnessed a consistent display of interests in the administration and funding of African education.

2.0 Pre-colonial/Traditional-Indigenous Education

Pre-colonial/ traditional-indigenous education in Sierra Leone was essentially an 'education for living'. It was largely informal and its main purpose was to train the youth for adulthood within the society. They learned by living and doing. In the homes and on the farms they were taught the skills of the society and the behavior expected of its members. This diffused pattern of traditional-indigenous education formed an integral part of the total process of socialization by which the younger members of the society acquired acceptable codes of behavior and the process of socialization was effectively implemented in real-life situations. Thus education had no fixed venues such as the classroom or the laboratory.
 There was no separate class of persons to whom such education was exclusively entrusted. In a sense, every adult was a teacher, although the more specialized forms of training were

traditionally entrusted to older members of the family circle, the village elders, senior ranks of the secret societies, the craftsmen and the diviners. Since part of this education was also received within the home, the span of training encompassed all the years from birth to post-adolescence.

The society regarded education as a means to an end and not as an end in itself. As Fafunwa (1971) noted, it was generally for an immediate induction into the society and a preparation for adulthood. Molding character and providing moral qualities were primary objectives in traditional-indigenous education. Moumouni (1968) indicated that sociability, integrity, honesty, courage, solidarity, endurance, ethics and above all the concept of honor were, among others, the moral qualities demanded, examined, judged and sanctioned, in a way which depended on the intellectual level and capacities of the child and adolescent.

Although the transmission of general knowledge was not systematic and organized as in modern education, nevertheless, it was effected through practical experience and through the oral teaching given to the child and adolescent in historical recitation and discussions. The community in general and the special community of the initiation camp in particular were the 'schools' of society. In these schools, the male youth learned to accept the authority of the elders and learned specific skills in hunting, fishing or cultivation. He also learned the wisdom of his ethnic group in stories and proverbs, forms of addresses and praises in honor of the chief and other distinguished figures of the culture. He learned what the right behavior in his community was and what his responsibilities were as the successor of the older generation.

Role tasks within the family circle were clearly defined. For example, the children were expected to perform certain domestic chores in strict conformity with their age and sex. Modes of greetings were scrupulously observed. For example, an obedient and good child does not hurl greetings at people from afar or pass adults without greeting them. All of these had a common design, namely "to ensure that the child does not deviate from the acceptable codes of conduct within the society and, furthermore, that the child's general conduct and demeanor should at all times reflect credit on his family" (Forde, 1975, cited by Brown and Hiskett, p. 73).

This process of socialization also embraced specific training for certain role tasks within the community at large. Education and work were much more directly linked. Every child was expected to acquire certain basic skills, which should enable him to participate fully in the social life of the community when he achieved full adulthood. There were a wide variety of skills, most of them of a functional character. The kind of skills a child acquired depended on a variety of circumstances, among which were the occupation of his parents, the locality in which he resided (farming community or fishing village) and his own natural propensities. In cases in which people relied on hunting, the training was related to those skills which "sharpened the senses of the youth and trained his responses to the stimuli of the environment" (Makulu, 1971, p. 2). In the same way, among the fishing community, a child was given the necessary orientation to make him an effective member of that particular group. This education would continue from childhood to adulthood, punctuated by intensified tests during points of crisis in the cycle of the individual in accordance with his physical and psychological development.

The effectiveness of the traditional-indigenous education was underpinned by its very close relationship and relevance to the people's ways of life. As Moumouni (1968) puts it, "it was through social acts (production) and social relationships (family life, group activities) that the education of the child or adolescent took place, so that he was instructed and educated simultaneously" (p. 29). It is perhaps unfortunate that the most significant aspect of traditional-indigenous education in Sierra Leone today is the fact that it is fast disappearing from the cultural scene.

The 1952 memorandum, 'Educational Policy in British Tropical Africa', was intended to design an educational system which could build and better the African cultural world. Further, the 1935 memorandum, 'Mass Education in Africa' championed the cause of the advocates when the equality of educational opportunities was extended to all members of the society, regardless of sex, ethnic and religious differences. The 1948 memorandum on "Education for Citizenship in Africa" affirmed the right of all individuals to access of educational facilities according to their capabilities in preparation for national leadership. It is therefore important for readers to bear this background of traditional-indigenous education in mind, in considering the effect upon Sierra Leone of colonial Western education.

2.1 Colonial Education

The arrival of the colonialists in West Africa in the fifteenth century brought a tradition of religious education and the church became prominent in the education of Africans. The Phelps-Stokes Commission reports carried weight and had considerable impact on the leading colonial powers in Africa. This was probably due to the international composition of the team, and the moral support received from the delegates at the Peace Treaty of World War I. Thus, the leading colonial powers undertook educational reform movements with differing national goals (Lebby, 1980).

The credit for the advent of colonial education in Sierra Leone goes entirely to the Christian missions. As Ayandele (1971) puts it "the real sowers were Christian missions who in the process enlisted the moral and financial support of their African adherents" (p.. 23). From the very beginning of the colony of Sierra Leone up to 1896 when vigorous expansion of European influence began, missionaries from Europe and America settled in Sierra Leone. One of the earliest missions to

Primary and Secondary Education in Sierra Leone

start operating in Sierra Leone was the Church Missionary Society in 1804 (Peterson, 1969). Within a decade, the mission had established a number of schools in Freetown and in the northern province among the Susu and Temne in Port Loko (Fyle, 1986). Between 1830 and 1950, with the arrival of other Christian Missionary Societies such as the Catholic Mission and the United Brethren in Christ, expansion of European influence and Western education began in earnest in the interior of Sierra Leone as several more primary and secondary schools and teacher education institutions were established (Sumner, 1964).

Ayandele (1971) described the primary aim of colonial education as to assist the people to know God in the manner prescribed by the Holy Scriptures, in other words to Christianize the people. But since the missionaries perceived from the beginning that the Gospel could not be divorced from the written word; that to establish the Gospel among the people, the latter must have Bibles which they must read, the use of education as a force which could aid them in quickly disseminating the knowledge of the Bible was considered necessary. These required some degree of general education and a relatively high degree of literacy education. Reading and writing skills in English were therefore obvious necessities and literary education became an essential part of their work.

The schools were regarded as evangelistic agencies and these were run and for the most part, financed by European missionary societies. Pupils were taught basic literacy and numeracy skills as well as considerable amounts of Christian doctrine. In effect, all the knowledge that was considered necessary and essential was the three R's with particular emphasis on the Bible and religious studies.

English, the language of the British, was used as the medium of instruction and the schools followed a basic academic curriculum similar to those used in British schools at the time. However, the missionaries felt that if Christianity was to be successfully established, they must give the converts more than the three R's; that his whole being should be changed by high quality education. Therefore the moral purpose of the school became an important purpose to the missionaries. As Fajana (1970) puts it "the secret spring of vital energy in a people was the morality which underlined the intelligence" (p. 104). The missionaries thus tried to "elicit ideas, evolve emotions and develop character in Africans, a people almost despaired of and dismissed as a miserable spectacle, deplorably wretched in body and mind" (Ayandele, 1971, p. 23). Thus it is evident that much as the primary aim of the founders of colonial education (the missionaries) was to put the souls of students in touch with God according to the prescription of Christianity, they sought to achieve other ends as well, one of which was to enable the beneficiaries to understand and be able to explain the world around them and acquire knowledge about other people.

The impetus given to education since the missionaries arrived came as a result of the fundamental aim of planning and establishing Christian institutions under the protection of British authorities (Rotimi, 1960). This was further intensified and increased, because, as Wilson (1963) reported, growing commerce and growth of even elementary government called for Sierra Leoneans competent to keep ledgers, undertake a variety of clerical, store-keeping and minor administrative tasks. The three R's therefore became the paramount pre-occupation of the 19th century schools and even to this day, they constitute the main focus, thus leaving a bookish imprint on the whole curriculum. But as the responsibility of introducing reforms into existing schools and of expanding education into the rural areas became the concern of the Christian missions, strategies used by the missions to convey their Christian message changed through time, but always involved some kind of schooling. One significant strategy which has survived as an important legacy of colonial education policy is mother tongue education: the teaching of the indigenous languages, which at the time, aimed primarily at enhancing the evangelizing process.

In the 1920's the British government began to accept

increasing responsibility, particularly for administration and finance of the educational system in Sierra Leone. The interest in the new role was reflected in the frequent enactment of Education Ordinances. The ordinances were designed to meet various aspects of a rapidly changing situation. In addition, various reports of educational surveys, commissions, and findings of thesis research brought to light the social, economic, political and cultural problems besetting the educational system in Sierra Leone.

In 1948 the governor commissioned Mr. H. Childs, commissioner in the Protectorate of Sierra Leone, to examine the measures and requirements necessary to achieve a substantial increase in the country's economic infrastructure relative to the prosperity and welfare of the people. Childs finished the investigation, suggesting a number of schemes to be undertaken by the central and local government agencies, including the districts, the Native Administration, and the rural area councils. Among other things, Childs proposed development of main communications, basic economic surveys, research, major schemes of production, and expansion of essential staff for the productive services which could be planned, and for the most part be executed, directly from the center (Childs, 1949).

Following his visit to Sierra Leone in 1953 during which he conducted field work for a dissertation in education at Michigan University, Coleson (1956) recommended the adoption of the fundamental education program designed by the United Nations Educational, Scientific, and Cultural Organization (UNESCO) as a viable proposition for alleviating Sierra Leone's existing educational malaise. Lebby (1980) identified the following objectives of the 1949 UNESCO publication: (a) skills of thinking and communication (reading and writing, speaking, listening and calculation) (b) vocational skills (such as agriculture and husbandry, building, weaving and other useful crafts, and simple technical and commercial skills necessary for economic progress) (c) domestic skills (such as the preparation of food and the care of children and of the sick) (d) skills used in self-expression in the arts and crafts (e) education for health through personal and community hygiene (f) knowledge and understanding of the human environment (economic and social organization, law and government) (g) knowledge of other parts of the world and the people who live in them (h) the development of qualities to fit men to live in the modern world, such as personal judgment and initiative, freedom from fear and superstition, sympathy and understanding for different points of view (i) spiritual and moral development – belief in ethical ideals, the habit of acting upon them, and the duty to examine the traditional standards of behavior and to modify them to suit new conditions.

In the task of making an appraisal of the different attempts that were made to clarify the object of colonial education in Sierra Leone, it is useful to briefly examine the reports of some of the important commissions on education in Africa. Of particular importance to Sierra Leone were the Phelps-Stokes Commission Report and the Cambridge Conference of African Education in 1952 (Makulu, 1971). The more significant points in the Phelps-Stokes Report were related to the importance of adaptation: that education should be adapted to the conditions of life was the prominent feature of the report.

For missions and churches, the most significant thing in the report was the strong plea it made for religious and moral education as the basis of a lasting education. The commission pointed in the direction education should take if it were to be of lasting value. Education in Africa needed to take into account the child's environment and the role in society which he has to play. The commission, in emphasizing the importance of the training of character, identified religious and moral instruction as priorities in the curriculum as it considered these to be of primary importance in the child's development.

The report of the West African group of the Cambridge Conference showed concern for the broad principles of education. As reported by Makulu (1971), the report showed a

Primary and Secondary Education in Sierra Leone

depth of understanding of the issues involved by broadly stating that the aim of education was to enable the child grow to full stature of a man, sound in mind and body. It also indicated that the child should acquire all the necessary skills according to his/her ability to enable himself/herself to be useful to the community. In other words, education should be a preparation for life so that the child can effectively take his/her place in the society.

The conference was convened to review the British Educational Policies as contained in the Advisory Committee recommendations on Education in Africa. The conference was based upon discussion of comprehensive reports collated by study groups sent to all British Tropical African colonies with the financial assistance of the Nuffield Foundation, under the sponsorship of the colonial office.

In 1924, two years after the recommendations of the Phelps-Stokes Commission Report, significant political and educational policies were made in Sierra Leone. Politically, it marked the beginning of a period of administrative unity, forged between the colony and the protectorate. By the dictates of the 1924 constitution, the two distinctive political regions previously ruled separately by the colonial office, for the first time, shared one legislative jurisdiction of the legislative council (Walker, 1963). Hence, the constitution provided for the appointment to the legislative council representation from the protectorate citizens, whose advice was deemed necessary on the formulation of government policies. Initially, in order to enable the people of the protectorate with a high *illiteracy* rate to understand the political system of the country, it was intended that priority should be given to educational development in the rural areas. Accordingly, in the same year, an educational ordinance was passed which spelled out rules and regulations governing the policies to be executed with regard to supply, status and training of teachers, inspection and supervision of schools, conduct of examination system, criteria for selecting and organizing curriculum content of school courses, and admission of children to schools without discrimination for reasons of sex, ethnic and religious differences (Board of Education of Sierra Leone Report, 1924).

Lebby (1980) noted that in 1925, the Advisory Committee issued a policy statement to the colonial office expressing the need for adaptation of education to the cultural views, aptitudes, occupations, and traditions of the diverse ethnic groups in the colonies. It was intended that such an educational program should be planned to produce not only consumers but also producers to promote personal, as well as national advancement. He further noted the committee recommended that it was the responsibility of the local administration in each dependency to promote the education of the whole community. This was to keep advancement at an equal pace for both the young and the adult citizens, in order to avoid, as far as possible, a generation gap in the society. Educational programs spelled out by the committee were not to be limited to only the conventional school system. Rather, they were to be designed in ways as to embrace an adult literacy campaign with the primary aim of integrating the school and the community.

However, this philosophy did not become popular because of the people's insatiable hunger for education of the academic type. For them, education symbolized power; it was seen as the door to the European's technological mysteries. Education was perceived as the escape route from manual work and from the old ethnic discipline. Far from being integrated with the economic, social and political facts of life, education was increasingly seen as a means of escape from them. To the people, education was the way up and out of the harsh subsistence economy from which most of them came. It was indeed an investment of the most rewarding kind. Thus it was regarded by them as a supplement to traditional life not as a means of transforming it. Little wonder then that Sierra Leoneans began to see education as an instrument of social and economic mobility always propelling the individual and his family with him in the

Primary and Secondary Education in Sierra Leone

upward direction. Education, therefore, as a missionary weapon of Christian proselytization and as a producer of subordinates for government and commercial service, was undoubtedly effective but was on the native peoples' terms (source?).

During their mission to Sierra Leone, members of the Phelps-Stokes Commission expressed grave concern about the inadequate educational provisions made for women and girls. The Advisory Committee endorsed the observation of Phelps Stokes Commission in their outline of the roles women should play in an African society such as that of Sierra Leone. The Committee indicated that women should not only preside in dwellings and direct or control the beginning of life, as was commonly expected of them by the African society. They should also hold vital forces that would make or unmake the individual and the social group in such matters as supply and preparation of well-balanced food; guaranteeing proper health and sanitary conditions of the homes; and the control of recreation of children. Therefore, the committee advised that due regard be made for adequate training of women, especially in such professional trainings, as teaching and nursing (Mayhew, 1938). The committee further warned that the education system of any society could be a curse rather than a blessing, if no provisions for women were made. It was maintained that female education should not be regarded as an isolated problem, but rather as an integral part of the whole education problem.

The Education Ordinance of 1924 provided for vocational and technical education in the country with equal treatment accorded to the general education system. It ruled that industrial schools up to standard III (grade 3) should be awarded government grants comparable to those given to regular elementary schools. The ordinance also contained a number of rules in regard to the professional and academic qualifications of teachers; their recruitment and classification; salary scales; teacher-pupil ratio; and the award of government grants per capita to schools. The Education Ordinance ruled that teachers should be required to take annual examinations for an award of certification and salary remuneration, measurable to their performances and level of qualification (Annual Report of the Board of Education of Sierra Leone, 1924).

It had never been expected that the application of missionary education might have a result very different from what had been anticipated. There had been little or no examination or analysis of what already existed in the colonized society itself. As Wilson (1963) indicated there was, indeed, a naive belief that Africa had no education and there was no understanding of the fact that education is part of the social organization of any society, whether or not that society has anything which might be recognized as a school.

The type of educational policies advanced by the colonial government was directly linked to the British policy of indirect rule, which in operational terms had conflicting interpretations. On the one hand, it sought to emphasize adaptation to the environment in order to create a basis for self-reliance and relevance for the indigenous people, while on the other hand, the type of education offered had to be functional within the perspective of the colonial administration, which needed to recruit low-level manpower with the considerable literacy skills to perform basic services within the colonial administration.

The colonial administration controlled the level of policy while the missions controlled the school curriculum. It was definitely a situation of both conflict and collaboration about goals, purposes and approaches in their separate efforts to undertake religious and secular evangelical crusades. It thus became a situation in which missions could only operate independently if they were able to be self-supporting, since there was general disagreement over what was educationally relevant. However, the growing cost of education made it difficult for missions to refuse financial assistance from government.

The Phelps-Stokes Commission did attempt to resolve some of the conflicts that had developed between the government and the missions in their approach to educational development. This was achieved by placing emphasis on the advantages and benefits of collaborative efforts among the colonial government, and the merchants as well as the missions, who also had segmented interests among the competing bodies (Sengova, 1982). However, there were various criticisms of colonial education. Kandel (1961), in his criticisms noted that the educational systems devised for the indigenous people have been nothing more than "transplantation of systems which have been developed under entirely different conditions and imposed without reference to the needs of the people" (p. 130). Ayandele (1971), described colonial education as "an edition of the world of white man, a palpable danger to the society in which Africans had lived, had moved and had their being from time immemorial" (p. 22). Watson (1994) stated that one of the most immediate effects of colonial involvement in many countries was, "unwittingly, to destroy existing indigenous education patterns, many of which were not only closely linked with cultural norms but also had a technical and vocational bias" (p. 86).

On the other hand, Wilson (1963) argued that although there has been criticism of the academic type of education introduced by the missionaries, it is criticism based on the wisdom of hindsight. He further asserts that it is difficult to see how these territories in the very first western contacts could ever have found an economic and administrative basis, let alone the spread of Christianity, without an education ground in the 3 R's and in a bookish curricula.

2.2 Post-Independence Education

Since the end of colonial rule, educational development in Africa has been a common target of criticism and heated debate. There has been a good deal of discussion about the pernicious effect of the 'colonial model' of education in independent Africa: its 'bookish' curriculum; its alienating and elitist orientation; its colonizing and imperialistic nature and its capacity to consume scarce resources at the expense of many, while benefiting only a few.

Sierra Leone achieved independence in April, 1961. At Independence, the idea of rapid expansion caught on very quickly. Primary enrollment experienced a phenomenal increase between 1960 and 1964. It rose from 70,429 in 1959/60 to 123,287 in 1964/65, with the most outstanding increase taking place during the first year of independence. In the 1960/61 and 1961/62 academic years, there was a 16.3% and 15.1% increase in enrollment figures. By 1964/65 the percentage increase took a dip to 4.6%, and by 1966/67 it was estimated at 2.8% (Educational Development, IDA Sector Study, 1979).

Banya (1991) makes the case that since independence, government's commitment to the expansion of the education system was facilitated by a program of granting recognition to new schools established by either philanthropic organizations (e.g. churches and local communities) or private organizations. Recognition meant the payment of salaries for qualified teachers, as well as covering operating and development costs, including the construction of a library or the development of curriculum units. This generous policy led to the rapid expansion of various types of schools, both primary and secondary.

With the attainment of political independence, national leaders of African countries made determined efforts to reform the educational system they had inherited from the colonial powers. Arianayagam (1970) pointed out that the rationale for such steps toward the renovation of the education system of the new nations was based on the following assumptions:
1. That the education of a new generation of citizens will foster in them the spirit of national consciousness to participate fully and willingly in the social and economic development plans of their nation.
2. That only an enlightened electorate can exercise political responsibility in decision-making process.
3. That a successful execution of plans for social and

economic development must be dependent upon intelligent cooperation of a society with skilled manpower.

The tremendous faith in education as the sole means of social and economic development has encountered serious criticism in recent years, so much so that one can easily trace a continuum of extreme optimism at the beginning of the decade of the sixties to the current trend of growing pessimism that characterizes much of the present discussions of educational issues. The national policies and programs after independence were all based on the actual circumstances of Sierra Leone, their general objectives and specific targets were also markedly inspired by international thinking and recommendations. Most important was the UNESCO Conference of African Ministers of Education in Addis Ababa, 1961, which agreed that:
1. The target date for achievement of six years of compulsory primary education should be 1980.
2. The secondary school intake should represent at least 30% of those completing primary school.
3. The widening gap between the educated and the illiterate masses should be narrowed.

Sierra Leone was represented at the conference and therefore committed itself to these recommendations. The resolution of the Addis Ababa conference conformed to the Universal Declaration of Human Rights in Article 26 of the United Nations, to which Sierra Leone became a subscriber after attaining political independence. According to this Article:
1. Everyone has a right to education. Education shall be free, at least in the elementary and fundamental stages. Technical and professional education shall be made generally available and higher education shall be equally accessible to all on the basis of merit.
2. Education shall be directed to the full development of the human personality and fundamental freedoms. It

shall promote understanding, tolerance, and friendship among all nations, racial, or religious groups and shall further the activities of the United Nations for the maintenance of peace.

At the same time, there was even some hope of reaching compulsory primary education in Sierra Leone by 1975. Anderson and Foster (1970) noted that the 1961 plan like other educational blue prints, was an array of prescriptions supported by largely tacit premises. The 1974/75 government education plan reflected a growing national awareness that a more realistic approach to planning education may be necessary. It seems, however, to be a bit overly pessimistic in dealing with the possibility of universal primary education. It warns that the goal of universality as an assumption should not be taken too far, and as Sengova (1982) observed, policymakers and planners may soon come to express what some have thought for some time, that universal primary education in the traditional school form is simply too costly to be achieved in the foreseeable future.

In the eagerness and rush to meet the target date of 1980, when it was hoped and resolved that every African state would have gained mass literacy, a new unexpected problem from policy-makers emerged. As Wood (1974) observed, it was the rapid expansion of quantitative formal education particularly at the primary education level. An in-depth research on student drop-outs in Sierra Leone conducted by UNESCO in 1966 pointed out the following:

1. The highest incidence of drop-out, from 40% to 50%, occurred between classes I and III.
2. The incidence of drop-out was higher in the rural areas than in urban schools.
3. It was higher among girls than boys.
4. Over-age children were more likely to dropout of school than those whose age corresponds to the normal class placement.

5. Schools which were staffed by unqualified teachers tend to have higher rates of drop-outs.
6. Where repetition rate was high, drop-out rate was also high.
7. Shortage of teachers and the improper education of serving teachers were significant causes of low productivity of education. (Smart, 1993)

The estimate of high wastage among the teachers, compounded by a high teacher-pupil ratio, gave cause for alarm among concerned policy-makers. To this end, the Ministry of Education resolved in the 1961/62 academic year to recruit expatriate teachers, many of whom were American Peace Corps and Canadian University Services overseas volunteer teachers (Report of the Ministry of Education, 1963).

The *illiteracy* rates of the rural population were correspondingly high and very little socio-economic development was taking place within the rural sector, and since the majority of the population are rural, invariably, any educational or socioeconomic development plan that neglects their interest, would be of little benefit to the country as a whole as far as total development is concerned.

Kelly's study in 1980 on the development of elementary education policy and practice in Sierra Leone elicits the following observations:

1. The inappropriate nature of the school curriculum, characterized by academic courses at the expense of practical and functional educational activities designed to satisfy the needs and aspirations of the people living in the society. He further indicated that such a system of education tended to turn out learned but inexperienced students in dealing with the problems of their own country.
2. That although there was a general national awareness and recognition of the educational right of women and girls, some lingering conservatism manifested itself among

parents, especially those of the Muslim and traditional African families. It appeared that more boys than girls were sent to school.
3. The vocational and technical schools were hardly used for the purposes for which they had been established and the poor image of vocational and technical education was certainly a contributing factor to the limited number of students who took advantage of the training offered in these schools.
4. The implementation process of the education policies also suffered for want of able-bodied leadership. There were rapid shifts due to political unrest, especially during the period between 1967 and 1972. The shifts often rendered policy implementers incapable of pursuing the results of previous policies, in that each new leader introduced policies which reflected their own personalities and educational philosophies.

These observations were also previously noted by Buck in his study in 1975. He pointed out that from a qualitative standpoint, no significant changes were either envisioned nor effected during this period.

One significant dimension of the policy development that emerged following Independence was that of the influence of the International agencies. These agencies have served as both advisory and financing bodies to most post-colonial developing countries in their attempt to provide an egalitarian and productive system of education and one that will promote inter alia, a rapid socio-economic development (Sengova, 1982).

Timity (1980) noted the following findings on the educational system:
1. The limited education resources (especially with the escalating costs of education) in Sierra Leone dictate or demand a complete rethinking of existing educational provision, not in terms of expanding numbers, but in

terms of a qualitative educational revolution(p.106).
2. There is evidence that the crisis is one of growing maladjustment between tradition bound educational systems and the rapidly changing world around them. Others concerned with education nationally and internationally, especially in countries of the "Third World," do realize the urgent need for educational reform which will reflect a broader and more realistic perception of education; with secondary school students developing skills which are transferable to jobs in an Agrarian Society (p.107).

These reports have to be seen against the realization that current school programs are neither adequate nor appropriate to the real needs of the population of Sierra Leone, nor indeed are they attainable within current levels of financial, human and material resources in the face of increasing school populations, the needs and demands of the unschooled and the needs of the urban populations of the Third World.

In summarizing his findings on the study of Sierra Leone's school curriculum in 1991, Nicol revealed that though there was a well defined educational philosophy and policy, there was also some evidence of discrepancy between the policy of the Ministry of Education, and the perceptions of the teachers and administrators relative to the mission and function of secondary education in Sierra Leone. The findings indicated that the opinions of the principals and teachers, who were charged with the responsibility of translating policy positions and statements into action, were not in harmony with policy prescriptions promulgated by the Sierra Leone Government, through the Ministry of Education.

A direction of change for education in Sierra Leone had been recommended in 1984 in a White Paper on education titled *'All Our Future'*. The recommendations were further affirmed in the *Mondeh-Fewry Report* of the 1980s, yet tangible steps were not taken to bring about change. The system of education presently in operation in Sierra Leone is known as the 6-3-3-4 system, tailored around the White Paper – *All Our Future*. The numbers 6-3-3-4 represent 6 years of formal primary schooling/education, 3 years of junior secondary schooling/education, 3 years of post-junior (senior) secondary schooling/education and 4 years of tertiary level education leading to a first degree.

In the period after 1985, the problems increased in the education sector. From an increase in enrolment of 6% between 1970 and 1985, enrolment in primary school declined by 2% on average in the period from 1985 to 1990 (Ministry of Youth, Education and Sport, 1996). The failure of the Government of Sierra Leone to service its debt with the World Bank resulted in the suspension of the Sierra Leone/IDA II education project between 1987 and 1992.

Primary and Secondary Education in Sierra Leone

1ST YEAR SECONDARY SCHOOL STUDENTS AT THE SIERRA LEONE GRAMMAR SCHOOL IN 1966
(*The author kneeling second from left*)

CHAPTER 3

Trends in Educational Policies

This chapter presents the findings to these questions:
1. What were the trends in educational policies during the colonial, post-colonial, and post-civil war eras?
2. What were the backgrounds to the trends which existed in those periods?

There were some common trends shown during the three periods under review: (a) international organizations had remarkable impact on the educational policy-making process and practice (b) since colonial times, English continues to be the language of instruction (c) student examination results have been used as proxy for measuring learning outcomes and (d) the centralized system of education existed since the colonial period, although the current Education Act specifies decentralization which is yet to be implemented.

At the same time, trends also show changes in the following: (a) movement from a predominantly grammar school type of education during the colonial and post-independence periods to a grammar school/vocational/technical education in the post-civil war period (b) changes in the age range of primary and secondary education during the colonial period (5-21 years) to lower ages (5-11, primary: 12-17, secondary) after independence and (c) student-teacher ratio was low during the colonial period as enrollment was small, but changed after post-independence and post-civil war periods to high ratios.

Primary and Secondary Education in Sierra Leone

3.0 Colonial

During the colonial period, education in Sierra Leone served largely as an entry point to the civil service for the few who could afford it. The recurrent policy statements stressed the need for education to be relevant to the needs of the indigenous population. Yet, as Sengova (1982) indicates, the Christianizing efforts of the missionaries, who were mainly involved with the running of the schools, clearly contradicted this intention. The schools were regarded as an evangelistic agency and these were run, for the most part, financed by European missionary societies. The colonial administration controlled the policies while the missions controlled the school curriculum. The fact that the education offered individual employment benefits outside the traditional sector made the 'academic-religious' curriculum relevant for those who were benefiting from it. Both local and international forces had a remarkable impact on the educational policy-making process and practice in Sierra Leone during the colonial period.

In the 1920's the British government began to accept increasing responsibility, particularly for administration and finance of the educational system in Sierra Leone. The interest in the new role was reflected in the frequent enactment of Education Ordinances. The Education Ordinance of 1924 provided for vocational and technical education in the country with equal treatment accorded to the general education system. It ruled that industrial schools up to standard III (grade 3) should be awarded government grants comparable to those given to regular elementary schools. The ordinance also contained a number of rules regarding the professional and academic qualifications of teachers, their recruitment and classification, salary scales, teacher-pupil ratio, and the award of government grants per capita to schools. The Education Ordinance ruled that teachers should be required to take annual examinations for an award of certification and salary remuneration, measurable to their performances and level of qualification (Annual Report of the Board of Education of Sierra Leone, 1924).

The 1922 Phelps-Stokes Commission Report influenced the Advisory Committee to facilitate the introduction of a number of British educational policies in Sierra Leone (Coleson, 1956). Basically, the aims of education as implied in the Phelps-Stokes Commission recommendations and endorsed by the Advisory Committee, were to foster: preservation and transmission of the cultural heritage of the past; ability to cope with the existing problems and a sense of preparation for the future. As described by Lebby (1980), the 1952 Cambridge Conference launched follow-up studies to examine the extent to which British educational policies had been implemented in tropical African dependencies such as Sierra Leone. He also indicated that the 1952 Educational Ordinance made provision for the administration of education at both central and local levels. The administrative system was structured on a pattern which associated regional communities with educational work in their areas. The ordinance further enabled the indigenous authorities to take an increasing part in the support and control of primary schooling. The 1952 ordinance created the machinery of local education authorities. The native administrative offices, as well as the District Councils in each of the three provinces, were charged with the responsibility of exercising control over the schools but a large part of the initiative in setting up and running schools continued to rest on the shoulders of the missionary organizations.

However, the adaptation notions and practice seemed inconsistent with the structure of the national economic system introduced by the colonists. As Lebby (1980) observed, it was incongruent with the concept of cultural adaptation, and created three main divisive forces: (a) it perennially divided Africans along ethnic lines (b) it intended to entrench the traditional authorities who were strong advocates of the colonial regime and (c) it prevented meaningful political dialogue and socio-economic competition between the Africans and the Europeans, African intellectual elites, and graduates of the cultural adaptation

Primary and Secondary Education in Sierra Leone

education system.

3.1 Post-Colonial/Independence

At Independence in 1961, Sierra Leone inherited a British-type education system, aimed largely at the urban middle class. The system was biased toward academically gifted students. Most Sierra Leoneans were unable to access formal education or forced by circumstances to work before completing primary school. The education system became an elitist system that excluded the majority of the population. National education policies were formulated, and implemented by the Ministry of Education. The Minister of Education was the political head of the ministry. The Permanent Secretary and the Chief Education Officer provided administrative and professional leadership respectively.

The first major move towards planning educational development in Sierra Leone after independence was a conference sponsored by UNESCO in 1961, less than a month after Sierra Leone became independent. The topic was *Development of Education in Africa*. Operating under the guiding principle of expansionism, the most significant conclusion to be drawn from this conference was the decision to identify the year 1980 as the target date for the achievement of universal free primary education. During the 1970's, there was a gradual shift towards greater control by nationals in deciding on their educational priorities. There was a persistent call for national participation in educational development. This was most marked with the *Sierra Leone Education Review*, which stressed the participation of nationals, and this has been strengthened with every subsequent statement.

The Jomtien World Conference on Education in 1990 gave birth to the *'Education for All'* movement (Kallon, 1996) and further buttressed the arguments for changes to education in Sierra Leone. This trend facilitated the adoption of the 6-3-3-4 system of education by the government in 1993 as a bold attempt to move the country away from a predominantly grammar school type of education, which takes neither the varied talents of the students nor the socioeconomic needs of the country into account. The establishment of the *National Commission for Basic Education* in 1993, the 1995 *New Education Policy for Sierra Leone*, and the *Education Master Plan* in 1997 can all be traced back to the *Education for All movement*. Following the Education Act of 1964, there were no policies embedded in the legal framework until the substantial post-war reforms.

3.2 Post-Civil War

Disparities are wide across different groups in terms of access to schooling and public spending on education. Female children, rural children and those in poorer households have reduced access to schooling. In many rural areas, attending primary school is still associated with the impediments of distance, affordability, and opportunity cost; attending junior secondary school remains difficult, and attending senior secondary school is almost impossible. The *Complementary Rapid Education for Primary Schools* (CREPS) system was instituted by the Ministry of Education in the 2000/01 school year to enable the many individuals aged 16 years and older who had their education disrupted by the long civil war to resume schooling. CREPS has started to be phased out as the backlog of war-affected children is absorbed into formal education.

After the war, the legal environment underwent substantial reforms, and between 2001 and 2004, the two important educational acts passed in 2004 that directly affect the primary and secondary education sector were:
1. *Education Act* – This replaced the Education Act of 1964 and outlines the structure of the education system, management and control, and the role of various actors in the system including local authorities. The major points include the legalization of the 6-3-3-4 education

system; and free and compulsory basic education. Ultimate authority for management and control of schools lies with the Minister of Education, but school management committees and board of governors will manage primary and secondary schools respectively. (Government of Sierra Leone, 2004)
2. *Local Government Act* – Under this act, local councils and local governments were established which marks the decentralization in education after 30 years of centralized governance. The management and supervision of basic education are transferred from central to local governments. (Government of Sierra Leone, 2004)

The *School Management Councils* are responsible for the day-to-day activities of government and government-assisted primary schools. According to the Education Act of 2004, the members of a school management council are the head teacher, the inspector of schools or his or her representative, the proprietor's representative, the chairman of the Community Teachers Association, the traditional ruler of the village, or area concerned, a female member or representative of the Chiefdom Education Committee, and a prominent educator. The board of governors manages government and government-assisted junior secondary schools. The Education Act mandates the minister of education to appoint six members of the board of governors including the chairman. With the approval of the Minister, four members are nominated by the proprietor of the school and one member by the local authority in which the school is located. The other members are the school principal and an ex-student.

Since colonial times, English has been and continues to be the language of instruction at both the primary and secondary levels of schooling. For primary grades 1 and 2, however, the medium of instruction can be both the community language and English. So that the national languages are not completely lost, the education policy encourages the teaching of national languages throughout the school system. The ingredient that has most contributed to the revitalization and rapid recovery of the Sierra Leone education system is the government's commitment to it. The Education Act of 2004 requires all children to complete basic education – 6 years of primary school and 3 years of junior secondary school (JSS). This poses an even greater challenge than universal primary education because the junior secondary school gross completion rate was only 31 percent in 2004/05 (World Bank, 2006). The current major policy objectives are to ensure 9 years (6 years of primary plus 3 years of junior secondary schooling) of basic education for all and to fully implement the new 6-3-3-4 structure with its strong scientific and vocational orientation, focusing on quality, relevance, and gender equalities.

Notwithstanding the many and varied financial constraints, the government in 2001 took on the challenge of providing free basic education, starting initially with the primary grades for all students and for girls from the Eastern and Northern Regions at the junior secondary school level. The government introduced a double-shift system in urban areas as a temporary measure to address the rural-urban migration of school-aged individuals during and immediately after the civil war conflict and to accommodate the rapid increase in enrolments over the past few years. The shift system is largely an urban phenomenon and has led to a reduction in the number of instruction hours in the school day.

A major decentralization process is taking place that will transfer power and responsibility for the delivery of basic services to local governments. According to the 3-year decentralization schedule, school management will be devolved from Ministry of Education to local district, city, or town councils, a process that had begun with the 2005/06 school year. These schools were previously governed by local councils during the first period of decentralization in the 1960s and early 1970s (World Bank, 2006). The councils will have full control and supervision of all primary and junior secondary schools by 2009, including such functions as the recruitment and payment of teachers, the provision of textbooks and teaching materials, payment of school fee subsidies, and the rehabilitation and construction of schools. The role of the central ministry in providing basic education is to focus on policy making and monitoring the performance of the local governments.

THE FIRST SECONDARY SCHOOL IN SIERRA LEONE: THE SIERRA LEONE GRAMMAR SCHOOL FOUNDED BY THE CMS IN 1845

CHAPTER 4

Trends in Educational Practices

In this chapter, the findings are related to these two questions:
1. How and to what extent did these policies influence the educational practices and standards at the primary and secondary school levels?
2. How did these policies impact the human resource needs of Sierra Leone?

4.0 Student Enrollment

Table 4.1 Primary Schools

School Year	Students Enrollment	% of School Age Children	Student-Teacher Ratio
1960/61	81,881	25	29:1
1970/71	166,107	49	32:1
1980/81	258,260	63	29:1
1990/91	375,941	66	36:1
2000/01	659,503	87	44:1
2009/10	1,408,192	79	50:1

Source: Ministry of Education

Table 4.2 Secondary Schools

School Year	Students Enrollment	% of School Age Children	Student-Teacher Ratio
1960/61	6,265	21	16:1
1970/71	33,318	27	22:1
1980/81	65,150	37	25:1
1990/91	71,282	43	26:1
2000/01	83,513	61	29:1
2009/10	133,597	52	35:1

Source: Ministry of Education

Figure 4.1

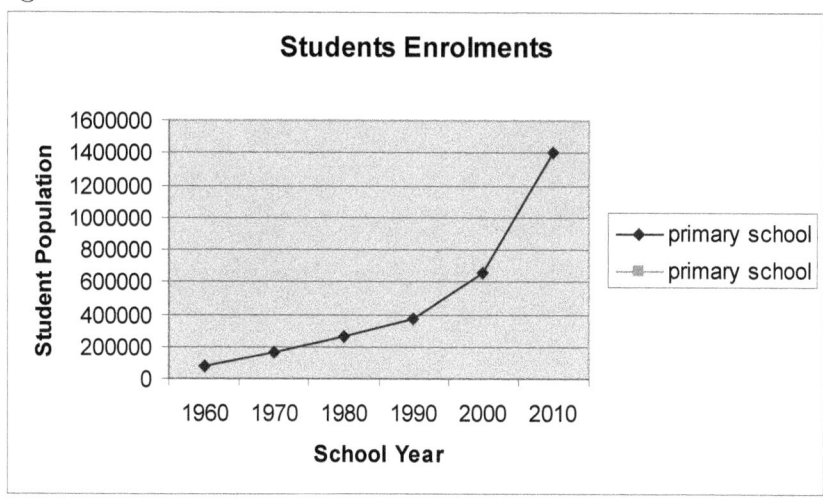

Figure 4.2

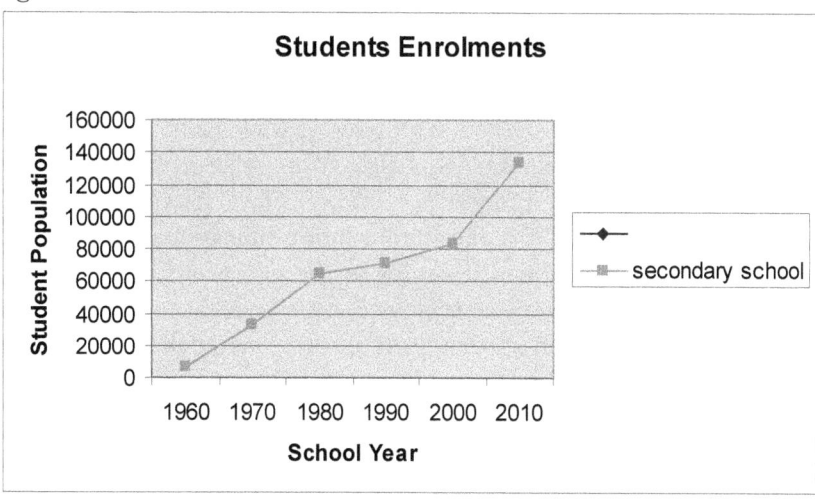

Figure 4.3

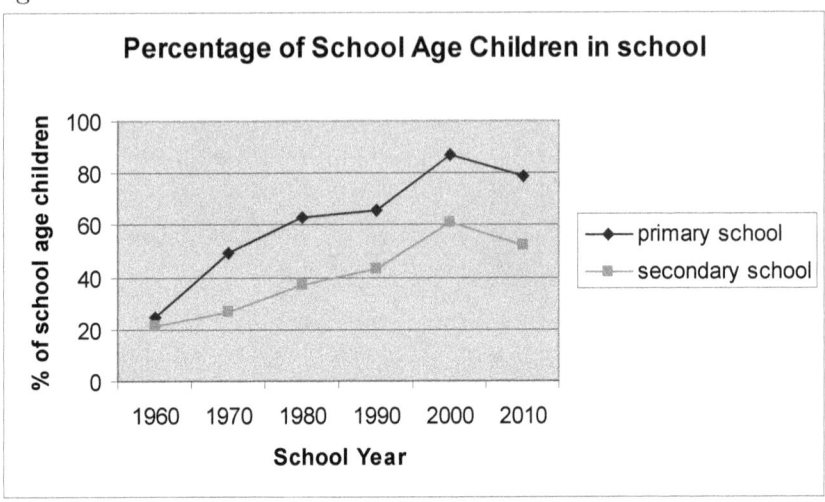

During the colonial period, the age range at the primary and secondary school levels was considerably mixed. Up to the 1950's, it was not uncommon to find students in the elementary schools with a cross section of ages varying from 5 to 21 years (Lebby, 1980). Nonetheless, much improvement was noticed in lowering the age range of students after independence. At independence in 1961, the first stage of education was provided in primary school, which begins at the age of six or seven and lasted for six or seven years. Secondary education, the second stage, was given in a variety of institutions such as secondary grammar schools, comprehensive schools, and trade schools. In 1961, fewer than 30% of children aged 5-11 years attended school and only 21% of children aged 12-16 years were in secondary schools. By 2010, 79% of children between 5-11 years were in school and 52% of children between 12-16 years were in school (Table 4.1 and 4.2).

The growth of primary and secondary education during the first ten years of independence was remarkably fast as reflected in the student enrollment (Tables 4.1 and 4.2). The number of primary school students more than doubled from 81,881 in 1960 to 166,107 in 1970 and 258,260 in 1980. In relative terms, the expansion was faster during the first ten years after independence than during the next decade. Expansion in secondary school enrollment was spectacular, increasing from 6,265 students in 1960 to 33,318 in 1970 and to 65,150 in 1980. Growth in primary school enrollment more than doubled, ten years after the civil war, from 659,503 in 2000 to 1,408,192 in 2010. During this same period also, secondary school enrollment increased by 60%.

In Sierra Leone, the official age ranges are 6-11 years for primary, 12-14 years for junior secondary school, and 15-17 years for senior secondary school. Based on the Population Census (2004), it is estimated that there were about 470,000 out-of-school children between ages 6 and 17, among whom 240,000 were 6-11 year olds, 90,000 were 12-14 year olds, and 140,000 were 15-17 year olds. The World Bank Report (2006) indicates that an analysis of student flow reveals a low survival rate, with only slightly more than 50 percent of primary school entrants completing the sixth year without repeating a grade. The report also noted that more than 70 percent of primary school completers go on to study at junior secondary schools, whereas only about half of the junior secondary school graduates move on to senior secondary schools.

The Ministry of Education's focus on expanding access to basic education for particularly the disadvantaged groups, such as girls and the primary and junior secondary school levels in the northern and eastern regions of the country, has led to a remarkable increase in student enrollments in the years following the end of the civil war. With the government's commitment and the introduction of the Free Primary Education Policy in 2001, student enrollments have increased rapidly at all levels. Enrollment doubled in primary school between 2000 and 2010 and increased significantly in junior secondary and senior secondary schools (JSS and SSS). According to the Inspectorate of the Ministry of Education, both junior secondary school and senior secondary school enrollments increased steadily between 2000/01 and 2009/10, with an annual growth rate of about 27 percent and 18 percent respectively. Secondary school enrollment rose from 83,000 in 2000/01 to 134,000 in 2009/10, almost doubling in ten years. The 2009/10 data shows an average of 50 students for every teacher at the primary level and 35 students per teacher in secondary schools. The increase in enrollment has contributed to overcrowding in schools and classes particularly in the Western Area due to increased migration to this area during the war. The Ministry of Education enacted policies limiting primary and junior secondary schools to a maximum enrollment of 1,500 students per school; senior secondary schools to a maximum enrollment of 1,200 students per school; class sizes to 50 students in primary schools, 30 students in junior secondary schools, and 25 students in senior secondary schools. Most secondary schools outside the Western Area have yet to reach the upper limit for school size, but the majority of schools in the Western Area are above the limit with class sizes of more than 60 students.

4.1 Teachers

Table 4.3 Percentage of Qualified Teachers

School Year	Primary Schools	Secondary Schools
1960/61	54	53
1970/71	40	68
1980/81	47	37
1990/91	41	33
2000/01	55	75
2009/10	47	38

Source: Ministry of Education

Figure 4.4

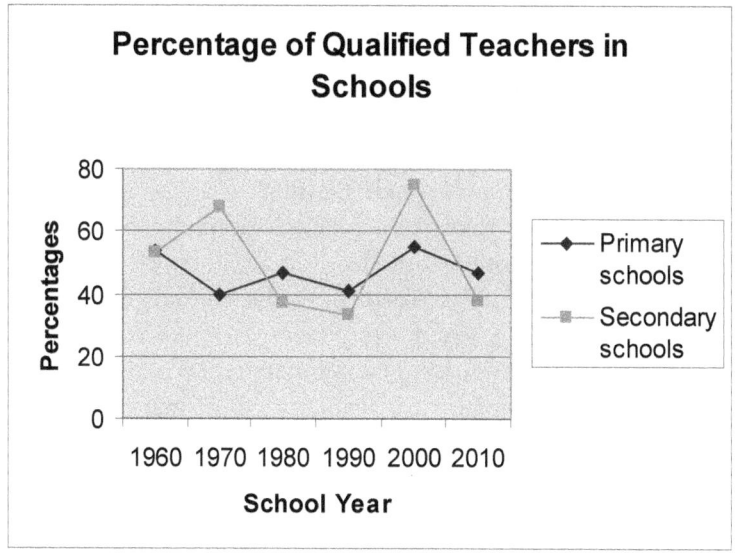

In 2009/2010, there were about 28,000 teachers in primary schools and 5,000 in secondary schools (Ministry of Education, 2010). 53% of these primary school teachers and 62% of the secondary school teachers are unqualified. The war left a deep scar on the teaching force. The large number of unqualified teachers is to some extent the consequence of the civil war. During the period of the civil war (1991-2001), many qualified teachers fled the country to safety and for employment in other countries. Many teachers are unqualified in the primary and secondary levels of schooling. Unqualified teachers are defined in Sierra Leone as those teaching at a level higher than appropriate for their academic qualification. Teachers who possess a degree but have not acquired any formal teaching certification are referred to as untrained. In order to be officially qualified to teach in Sierra Leone's primary or secondary schools, prospective teachers need to receive the relevant teacher certificates or advanced education degrees. Traditionally, primary school teachers attend teacher training colleges for three years after junior secondary school and are awarded the Teacher's Certificate. Junior secondary school teachers attend teachers' colleges, where studies lead to a Higher Teacher's Certificate and senior secondary school teachers must obtain a four-year bachelor's degree.

Teachers in secondary schools may be underutilized as most of them teach less than the expected minimum of 30 periods a week. On the other hand, primary school teachers are overstretched, as they perform both the administrative duties of a class teacher and teach every period of each school day. A major dilemma for educational planners and administrators is the problem of the quality of teaching in primary schools. The percentage of unqualified teachers especially in primary schools is alarmingly high with the rural areas suffering more from this problem, since most of the qualified teachers tend to gravitate towards urban areas.

4.2 Student Performance/Achievement

Since the colonial period, student examination results have been used as a proxy for measuring learning outcomes in primary and secondary education. During the colonial period, the duration of the elementary school course varied from 7 to 9 years. The students' chances of gaining entrance into secondary schools were heavily dependent upon the quality of their performance in the Selective Entrance Examination (originally referred to as Common Entrance) which was conducted once every academic year. Students could attempt the examination while they were in Senior Primary I or Senior Primary II, with outstanding students in Senior Primary I sent to the examination at the recommendation of the class teacher. However, during the 1960's, both Senior Primary I and II classes were abolished. Thus, the primary school course was reduced to 7 years duration with an age range of 5 to 12 years. By this kind of arrangement, students took the entrance examination at the completion of classes 6 and 7. Similarly, some class 6 (grade 6) students took the examination at the recommendation of the class teacher.

Normal duration of the secondary school course was 5 years, after which the students went for the School Certificate of the West African Examination Council (formerly called Senior Cambridge before 1961). A good result qualified the student for admission to the University of Sierra Leone, if they got an award of a government scholarship, since most parents could not afford to support their children toward higher education. Pursuance of secondary school education for two years after Form 5 (grade 12) was optional.

Sierra Leone does not have a student learning assessment system designed specifically to assess the entire education system, but there are plans to develop one. The country does have a public examination system that focuses on the assessment of individual students. Since 1995, all students at the end of class six (grade 6) are required to take and pass the National Primary School Examination (NPSE) designed by the West African Examinations Council (WAEC) to enable them to proceed to the secondary level. The secondary level is divided into two parts each of 3 years - JSS and SSS. Each part has a final examination: the Basic Education Certificate Examination (BECE) for JSS and the West Africa Senior School Certificate Examination (WASSCE) for SSS both administered by the West African Examinations Council (WAEC). The examination syllabi are produced by the West African Examinations Council (WAEC).

The current curriculum of primary schools emphasizes communication competence and the ability to understand and manipulate numbers. At the JSS level, the curriculum is general and comprehensive, encompassing the whole range of knowledge, attitudes, and skills. The core subjects: English, mathematics, science and social studies are compulsory for all students. At the SSS level, the curriculum is determined by its nature (general or specialist) or its particular objectives.

Table 4.4 Common Entrance/National Primary School Exams (NPSE)

School Year		Number of students who took the exams	Pass Rates (%)
1960/61	(Common Entrance)	9,063	32
1970/71	(Common Entrance)	14,033	62
1980/81	(Common Entrance)	20,920	56
1990/91	(Common Entrance)	24,708	55
2000/01 (NPSE)		20,189	93
2009/10 (NPSE)		97,394	74

Source: West Africa Examinations Council

The NPSE tests students in mathematics, English, verbal aptitude, quantitative aptitude and general studies (science and social studies). The tests are designed to be comparable from year to year. The result of this examination, including continuous assessment scores (weighted 10%), is used for placement into junior secondary school. A review of the number of students passing the NPSE showed that as standards have become more rigorous, the percentage of pass rate had decreased, although the system has been producing increased number of students passing the exam from 2000 to 2010.

As a result of the rapid increase in primary school enrollments and the abolishment of fees for examinations at the end of primary school, the number of students taking the NPSE greatly increased from about 20,000 in 2000 to 97,000 in 2010. The score required to pass the test is determined yearly by the Ministry of Education. It has been gradually increased as the number of candidates taking the examination increases. This, according to the Ministry of Education, is to regulate access to JSS on the basis of available space and to try to ensure that a greater percentage of those progressing to junior secondary school would be able to succeed in the program. The World Bank Report (2006) showed that the gross completion ratio in primary education was 65% in 2004/05, considerably short of the goal of 100%.

Table 4.5 Basic Education Certificate Exams (BECE)

School Year	Number of students who took the exams	Pass Rates (%)
1995/96	11,950	9
2000/01	18,347	39
2005/06	49,880	38
2009/10	73,501	50

Source: *West Africa Examinations Council*

In the BECE, each candidate is tested in eight subjects, four of which are compulsory (language arts, mathematics, science, and social studies). BECE papers are marked and standardized on a seven-point scale. A score of 1-4 is a credit, 1-6 is a pass, and 7 is a fail. An aggregate score is determined by summing six subjects: four compulsory, one prevocational, and one other subject. The cumulative assessment scores of the school constitute part of the final BECE scores with a weight of 20%.

The number of candidates who took the BECE increased more than 300% between 2000 and 2010, with an increase in pass rate from 38% to 50% (Table 4.5). The World Bank Report (2006) indicated that significantly fewer girls (35% of BECE candidates) than boys took the BECE.

SSS ends with the West Africa Senior School Certificate Examination (WASSCE). The number of candidates taking the WASSCE since 1995 has been increasing with more than 35,000 in 2010 (Table 4.6). Pass rates (defined as credits in four or more subjects) were extremely low, with only 26% passing the WASSCE in 2010 (Figure 4.5).

Table 4.6 West Africa Examination Council General Certificate Ordinary Level School Exams (WAEC/GCE – O Level) /West Africa Senior School Certificate Exams(WASSCE)

School Year	Number of students who took the exams	Pass Rates (%)
1960/61 (WAEC/School Certificate)	367	51
1970/71 (WAEC/GCE-O Level)	3990	10
1980/81 (WAEC/GCE-O Level)	6993	19
1990/91 (WAEC/GCE-O Level)	10,830	33
2000/01 (WASSCE)	11,273	29
2009/10 (WASSCE)	35,341	26

Source: *West Africa Examinations Council*

Figure 4.5

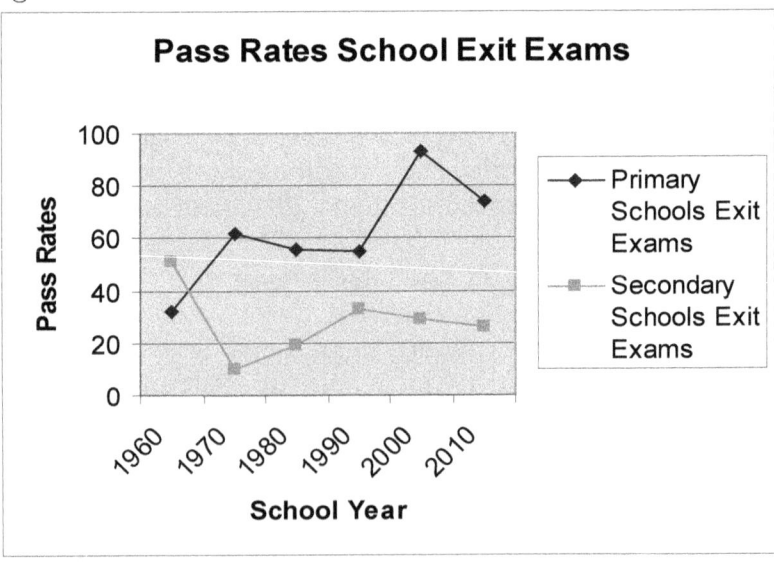

Primary and Secondary Education in Sierra Leone

Table 4.7 Primary Schools Demography by Regions (2009/10)

Regions	Number of Schools	Number of Students	% of School Age Children	Student-Teacher Ratio	% of Qualified Teachers
North	1961	490,848	67	52:1	42
South	1332	348,318	77	55:1	40
East	1105	323,337	74	51:1	45
West	530	245,689	85	43:1	59

Source: Ministry of Education

Although the northern region of the country has the highest number of students enrolled in primary schools, the western area (which includes the capital city and the national government offices) has the highest percentage of primary school age children (Table 4.7). The southern region has a high student-teacher ratio (55:1) as teachers find employment in the western area and places of comparatively better facilities and living conditions.

Table 4.8 Secondary Schools Demography by Regions (2009/10)

Regions	Number of Schools	Number of Students	% of School Age Children	Student-Teacher Ratio	% of Qualified Teachers
North	84	24,640	31	38:1	43
South	68	24,666	34	37:1	34
East	65	24,090	45	51:1	33
West	65	60,201	43	33:1	40

Source: Ministry of Education

Figure 4.6

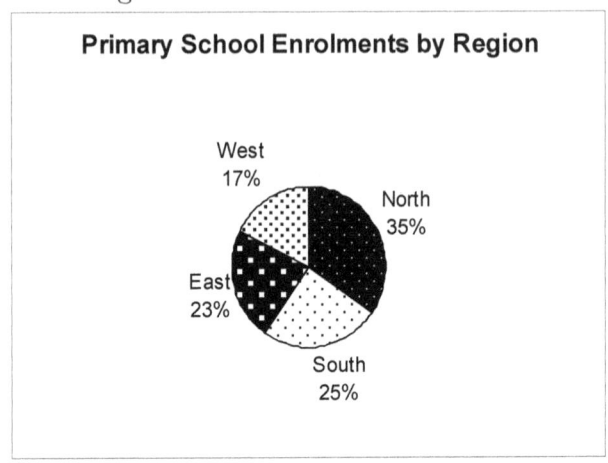

Figure 4.7

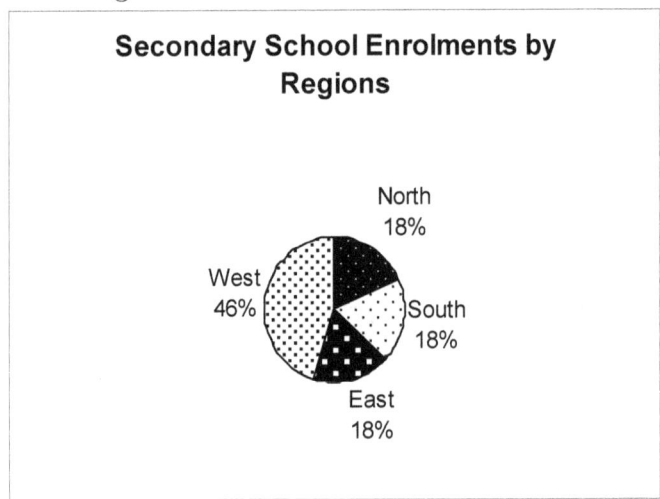

In secondary education, the western area has the highest number of enrolled students with a comparatively low student-teacher ratio (Table 4.8).

Figure 4.8

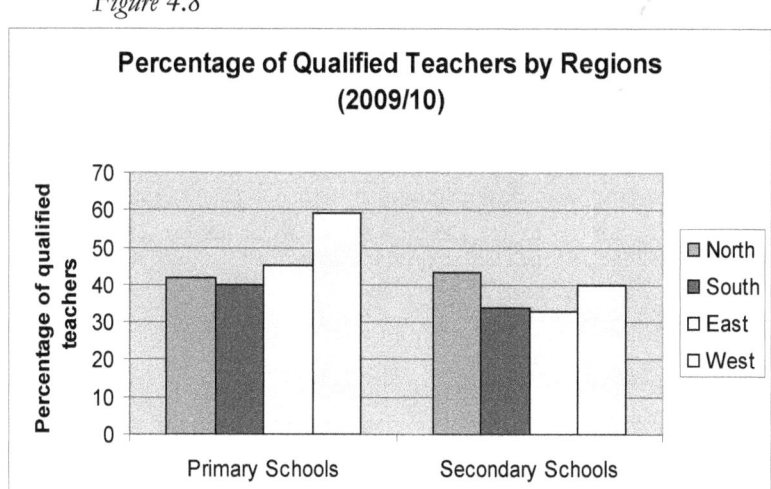

Figure 4.8 shows the number of qualified teachers by region. The share of qualified teachers in primary schools was less than 50% in all the regions except the Western Area. The problem is similar at the secondary level where there are still many unqualified teachers.

Table 4.9 National Primary School Exams Pass Rates by Region (2009/10)

Regions	Pass Rate (%)
North	73
South	76
East	75
West	74

Source: West Africa Examinations Council

Table 4.10 Basic Education Certificate Exams Pass Rates by Region (2009/10)

Regions	Pass Rate (%)
North	41
South	43
East	53
West	62

Source: *West Africa Examinations Council*

Table 4.11 West Africa Senior School Certificate Exams Pass Rates by Region (2009/10)

Regions	Pass Rate (%)
North	29
South	26
East	23
West	29

Source: *West Africa Examinations Council*

Figure 4.9

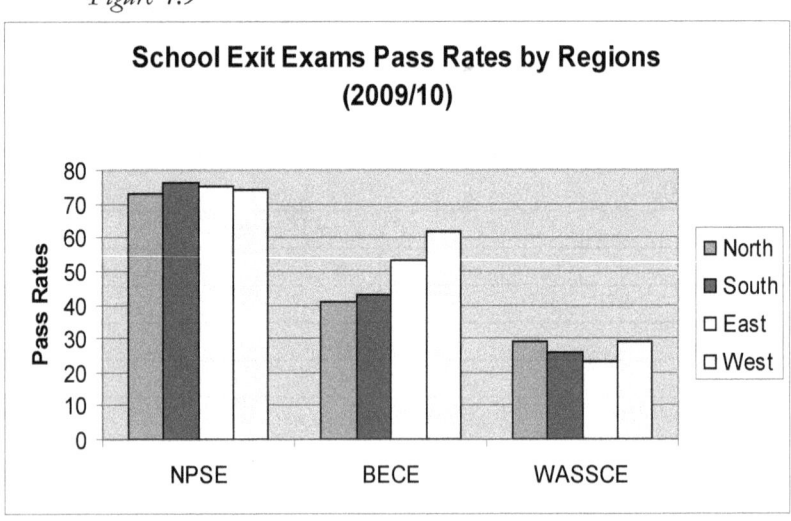

In 2010, there were significant regional differences in NPSE pass rates (Figure 4.9), with the Southern Region having the highest rates and the Northern Region the lowest rates. Almost half of all BECE candidates were from the Western Area in 2010, and it is known that many candidates from other areas go to the Western Area for junior secondary schooling because the schools are believed to be of better quality. Among the four regions, the Western Area had the highest pass rate at 62% in 2010, followed by the Eastern Region at 53%; and the Southern and Northern Regions had the lowest pass rates at 43% and 41% respectively (Table 4.10). In 2010, all the regions had very low WASSCE pass rates (between 23% and 29%; Table 4.11).

CHAPTER 5

Current Perceptions

This chapter presents the responses of interviews conducted with school administrators, primary and secondary school teachers from the four regions of the country in 2008 and 2010. The interviews were conducted to obtain the perceptions of stakeholders in education on the needs to improve education in Sierra Leone. Below are tables showing the questionnaire responses.

Table 5.1 Primary Schools Administrators' Perception of Policy Implementation, Teaching and Learning: N=20

School Administrators	Strongly Agree		Agree		Not Sure		Disagree		Strongly Disagree	
	#	%	#	%	#	%	#	%	#	%
School policies are clearly defined.			14	70	6	30				
School curriculum meets the needs of the country.	5	25	15	75						
Learning support materials are readily provided.					6	30	7	35	7	35
Adequate room/space for teaching and learning.			14	70			6	30		
School environment is conducive to learning.			12	60			8	40		

Teacher turnover rate is low.			6	30			14	70	
There is a problem of teacher shortage.	8	40	8	40			4	20	
Teacher moral is low.	13	65	7	35					

Table 5.2 Secondary Schools Administrators' Perception of Policy Implementation, Teaching and Learning: N=20

School Administrators	Strongly Agree		Agree		Not Sure		Disagree		Strongly Disagree	
	#	%	#	%	#	%	#	%	#	%
School policies are clearly defined.	5	25	15	75						
School curriculum meets the needs of the country.			15	75	3	15	2	10		
Learning support materials are readily provided.					6	30	12	60	2	10
Adequate room/space for teaching and learning.			6	30	2	10	3	15	9	45
School environment is conducive to learning.					9	45	6	30	5	25
Teacher turnover rate is low.			9	45			2	10	9	45
There is a problem of teacher shortage.	3	15	15	75			2	10		
Teacher moral is low.	5	25	15	75						

A large majority of the school administrators (70% in primary schools and 100% in secondary schools) surveyed agreed that the policies on schools were clearly defined but almost 70% of them complained that the learning materials needed to support instruction were not readily available. As one school administrator noted in her response, "there is lack of teaching and learning materials, computers and other facilities to support the ideals of the 6-3-3-4 education". Overcrowding in classrooms was a common problem in schools in the Western Area due to the massive migration to the capital city during and after the war. As such, effective teaching and learning were undermined. All the school administrators indicated that there was a problem of teacher shortage in both primary and secondary schools. All the respondents also indicated that because of poor salary and conditions of service, teacher moral was extremely low. The major constraint indicated by most school administrators, especially those at the secondary level, was lack of qualified and trained teachers.

70% of primary school administrators and 55% of secondary school administrators agreed that teacher turnover rate was high. The higher turnover rate in primary schools can be partly attributed to low salaries for primary school teachers who then decide to pursue further studies to improve their qualifications for better salaries. The responses from school administrators showed that teacher shortage was a major problem more in secondary schools than primary schools. One of the reasons was that in secondary schools, stricter adherence was emphasized on employing qualified teachers.

Primary and Secondary Education in Sierra Leone

Table 5.3 Primary Schools Administrators' Perception of Policy Implementation, Teaching and Learning by Regions (North, South, East, and West): N=20

School Administrators	# Agree				# Not Sure				# Disagree			
	N	S	E	W	N	S	E	W	N	S	E	W
School policies are clearly defined.	1	4	4	5	4	1	1					
School curriculum meets the needs of the country.	5	5	5	5								
Learning support materials are readily provided.					2	1	2	1	3	4	3	4
Adequate room/space for teaching and learning.	5	4	5							1		5
School environment is conducive to learning.	3	2	5	2					2	3		3
Teacher turnover rate is low.	2	2	2						3	3	3	5
There is a problem of teacher shortage.	5	3	5	3						2		2
Teacher moral is low.	5	5	5	5								

Table 5.4 Secondary Schools Administrators' Perception of Policy Implementation, Teaching and Learning by Regions (North, South, East and West): N=20

School Administrators	# Agree				# Not Sure				# Disagree			
	N	S	E	W	N	S	E	W	N	S	E	W
School policies are clearly defined.	5	5	5	5								
School curriculum meets the needs of the country.	3	4	4	4	2	1					1	1
Learning support materials are readily provided.					2	1	2	1	3	4	3	4
Adequate room/space for teaching and learning.	3	1	2		1		1		1	4	2	5
School environment is conducive to learning.					3	3	2	1	2	2	3	4
Teacher turnover rate is low.	3	3	3						2	2	2	5
There is a problem of teacher shortage.	4	5	4	5					1		1	
Teacher moral is low.	5	5	5	5								

The survey showed that there is a consensus among all the school administrators in the western region that there was inadequate classroom space for students. Schools in the western region are experiencing overcrowding because of the migration of students from other regions during and immediately after the civil war. Also, 100% of primary and secondary school administrators in all the four regions surveyed indicated that teacher moral was low and a large majority was concerned about high teacher turnover rate. In addition, both primary and secondary school administrators from the northern and eastern parts of the country gave more negative responses to shortage of teachers.

Table 5.5 Primary Schools Teachers' Perception of Policy Implementation, Teaching and Learning: N=60

chers	Strongly Agree		Agree		Not Sure		Disagree		Strongly Disagree	
	#	%	#	%	#	%	#	%	#	%
ool policies are rly defined.	12	20	8	13			40	67		
ool curriculum ts the needs of country.					27	45	33	55		
rning support erials are readily ided.							41	68	19	32
quate room/space eaching and ning.	23	38	8	14			9	15	20	33
ool environment is ducive to learning.	14	24	17	28			29	48		
re are ortunities for staff elopment.							30	50	30	50
aries are adequate eachers.							35	58	25	42
dents regularly nd school.			22	37	20	33	18	30		
ents are involved eir children's cation.			45	75			15	25		

Table 5.6 Secondary Schools Teachers' Perception of Policy Implementation, Teaching and Learning: N=60

Teachers	Strongly Agree		Agree		Not Sure		Disagree		Strongly Disagree
	#	%	#	%	#	%	#	%	#
School policies are clearly defined.	28	47	20	33			6	10	6
School curriculum meets the needs of the country.			36	60	12	20	12	20	
Learning support materials are readily provided.			10	17			50	83	
Adequate room/space for teaching and learning.	10	17					40	66	10
School environment is conducive to learning.	12	20	25	42			16	27	7
There are opportunities for staff development.			19	31			16	27	25
Salaries are adequate for teachers.					1	1	14	24	45
Students regularly attend school.	5	8	15	25			40	67	
Parents are involved in their children's education.			40	66	16	27			4

100% of primary school teachers and 69% of secondary school teachers affirmed that there was no opportunity for staff development. All of the teachers in the survey were not satisfied with their jobs because of inadequate salaries and incentives. There were however some positive responses to changes in the educational policies in the past ten years. These included the increase in enrollment of girls in schools and free basic education (primary through junior secondary schools).

Majority (67%) of the primary school teachers surveyed indicated that the school policies were not clearly defined whereas only 20% of the secondary school teachers said that the school policies were not clearly defined. Reasons for this variance can be attributed to the high percentage of unqualified teachers in primary schools who might not understand school policies and/or lack of professional development that exposes primary school teachers to school policies.

In their responses to suggestions for improvement, the teachers as well as the school administrators surveyed, requested (a) increase in salaries (b) improvement in conditions of service (c) more opportunities for staff development (d) building of more schools to reduce the large classroom sizes in the Western Area and (e) more autonomy for school administrators to manage schools.

Table 5.7 Primary Schools Teachers' Perception of Policy Implementation, Teaching and Learning (North, South, East, and West): N=60

Teacher	# Agree				# Not Sure				# Disagree			
	N	S	E	W	N	S	E	W	N	S	E	W
School policies are clearly defined.	3	5	4	8					12	10	11	7
School curriculum meets the needs of the country.					13	5	9		2	10	6	15
Learning support materials are readily provided.									15	15	15	15
Adequate room/space for teaching and learning.	11	10	10						4	5	5	15
School	11	7	10	3					4	8	5	12

Teacher	# Agree				# Not Sure				# Disagree			
	N	S	E	W	N	S	E	W	N	S	E	W
environment is conducive to learning.												
There are opportunities for staff development.									15	15	15	15
Salaries are adequate for teachers.									15	15	15	15
Students regularly attend school.	8	6	8		4	5	3	8	3	4	4	7
Parents are involved in their children's education.	12	9	14	10					3	6	1	5

Table 5.8 Secondary Schools Teachers' Perception of Policy Implementation, Teaching and Learning (North, South, East, and West): N=60

Teacher	# Agree				# Not Sure				# Disagree			
	N	S	E	W	N	S	E	W	N	S	E	W
School policies are clearly defined.	10	12	12	14					5	3	3	1
School curriculum meets the needs of the country.	6	10	8	12	8	1	2	1	1	4	5	2
Learning support materials are readily provided.	1	2	2	5					14	13	13	10

Adequate room/space for teaching and learning.	2	4	4						13	11	11	15
School environment is conducive to learning.	11	9	8	9					4	6	7	6
There are opportunities for staff development.	2	5	4	8					13	10	11	7
Salaries are adequate for teachers.								1	15	15	15	14
Students regularly attend school.	6	5	6	3					9	10	9	12
Parents are involved in their children's education.	8	9	10	13	5	6	4	1	2		1	1

All the primary and secondary school teachers surveyed in the four regions indicated that their salaries were inadequate and a large majority complained about the lack of learning support materials and opportunities for staff development. It is noteworthy that most secondary school teachers across all the four regions agreed that the curricula met the national needs. However, none of the primary school teachers in the four regions agreed with this idea. Majority of the primary school teachers who did not agree were from the southern and western regions of the country.

As a result of the poor performance of pupils in the 2008 BECE and WASSCE, the Gbamanja Commission of Inquiry, set up by the President, Dr. Ernest Koroma, made recommendations including the following:

1. Modification of the 6-3-3-4 system of education to include a compulsory early child component and an extension by one year of the duration of senior secondary school to 6-3-4-4. (Immediate)
2. Free and compulsory primary education in both policy and practice. (Immediate)
3. Establishment of Teaching Service Commission with a review of the conditions of service of teachers as a top priority action. (Immediate)
4. Establishment of the National Institute of Education, Training and Research (NIETAR) by legislation as a semi-autonomous specialized agency for curriculum development, teacher development and educational research, with a study of special needs education as a priority. (Immediate)
5. Phasing out of the two-shift system in secondary schools within a period of three years. (Immediate)
6. Reduction of the number of examination subjects from 9 to 7 subjects for BECE and WASSCE in conformity with the decisions of the other West African countries. (Immediate)
7. Reduction of class sizes with 50 and more pupils. (Short term)
8. Training of all untrained and unqualified teachers throughout the country through well structured training programs. (Short term)
9. Training of all Heads of schools and colleges on educational administration and management and in computer application. (Short term)

(Gbamanja Commission Report, 2012)

CHAPTER 6

Analysis

This chapter analyses the findings of the effects of educational policies on primary and secondary education in Sierra Leone. The analysis focuses on generalizing the quantitative data in chapter four that shows observable changes on practices and standards in the areas of student enrollment, academic achievements, drop-outs and teacher shortage. It also involves trends in policy changes from the colonial period to present.

The findings indicate that as Sierra Leone emerged from a brutal civil war that lasted ten years (1991-2001) and destroyed most of the country's social, economic, and physical infrastructure, the war left a multitude of scars in the education sector: devastated school infrastructure, severe shortage of teaching materials, overcrowding in many classrooms in safer areas, displacement of teachers, disorientation and psychological trauma among children, poor learning outcomes, and weakened institutional capacity to manage the system. Since the end of the civil war, there has been a growing demand for education and the subsequent expansion in the system. However, the expansion at the primary level has not been matched by similar provision at the post-primary level, which has resulted in an educational bottleneck compounded by a relatively sluggish economy in which youth unemployment and underemployment are high. But during the colonial period, because of the low student enrollment at the primary level, the secondary level was able to absorb students entering from the primary school level.

6.0 School Enrollment

Education for All (EFA) is now defined by the international community as quality universal education (Wang, 2007). It is clear that the achievement of EFA in Sierra Leone by 2015 will be very challenging. It will be a long-term process, requiring tenacious effort, strong and sustained political will and perhaps brighter economic prospects. 20% of children between the ages of 6 and 11 remain out of school. Besides, enrolling students in school is not enough. It takes 6 years for children to complete primary school (without taking into account repetition), which means that all suitably aged children should have been enrolled in primary grade 1 by 2009 if they were to complete grade 6 in 2015. Enrolling children in primary grade 1 is only the first step; ensuring that children can complete primary education is another critical step. There exists a large and ever expanding primary school system of very mixed quality, with a high drop-out rate, seldom catering for more than half of the primary school age group, crippled by excessive enrollment at the lower end.

The issues of EFA are about the poor and the disadvantaged and the aim of the educational policy should therefore be to give every child a chance of developing his/her inherent potential. The typical response to this overwhelming pressure of popular demand for universal primary education has been to spread sparse resources (such as classrooms, teachers, and books) thinner and thinner over more students. Therefore these educational resources are not used effectively to educate the children in an educational system that produces high statistics of drop-outs and repeaters.

The findings also show that the education provided is mainly intended to prepare students to pass examinations. Since the colonial period, schools are judged on the basis of the performance of their students at such examinations as the NPSE BECE and WASSCE. If a student does not pass the school leaving examination, the whole education is judged as a failure and in a very real sense, it could be the end of any career ambitions including employment.

6.1 Academic Achievement

The quality and relevance of the examination system should be reviewed and analysis of the results of these examinations should go beyond just pass rates, which are more suitable for deciding student advancement than for determining what students have learned and how well they have done so. The West Africa Examination Council (WAEC) examinations are designed for selecting individual students to be promoted to the next level of the education system, not for evaluating the system itself, a condition inherited from the colonial administration. The pass rates do not indicate the level of education achieved by students, because the rates are affected by the available space in the next level of the system. A true assessment system should be able to determine whether the education system is performing well in terms of learning outcomes, the strengths and weaknesses of the system, determining whether the curricula are well designed and identifying factors associated with learning outcomes.

Literacy was defined in the population census of 2004 as being able to read and write in any language. Of those aged 10 years and older, only 39% are literate (Statistics Sierra Leone, 2004). As indicated by the Sierra Leone Integrated Household Survey (SLIHS, 2004), it takes about six years of successful primary schooling to become literate, highlighting the importance of completing primary education. There is a highly selective academic secondary school system, too often conventional, geared to the requirements of university entrance. There is inadequate provision for (non-academic) post-primary vocational education, an area of training which has evoked little enthusiasm from those who might have profited by it and only lip service from the academically educated leaders who should have provided it.

A relatively small percentage of primary school leavers has an opportunity for post-secondary education and a very high percentage of students leave school after only 1, 2 or 3 years. This means that money is being spent every year, out of inadequate resources, on children who stay at school for too short a time to gain any lasting benefit for themselves and society. This is a serious problem both to those students and society. To the students who drop out and their parents, it is failure, with its high financial costs and psychological pain, especially in an underdeveloped society in which education is the most important factor in upward social and economic mobility. For society, the cost can be immense, since successful completion of primary and/or secondary education constitutes reasonable levels of attainment of different strata of productive contribution to society.

Resources spent on those students who do not reach the minimum are therefore largely frittered away. Sierra Leone is a country where resources are scarce and therefore not to be wasted. High dropout and repetition rates are key sources of waste. The surge of student enrollment in primary school, which started after independence and escalated after the war, granted many children an opportunity to obtain education but the education service delivery has struggled to cope with the sudden and huge expansion of the system. This has resulted in a serious lack of qualified teachers, classrooms, and teaching materials which might have contributed to the low survival and high repetition rates in primary schools. As such, the challenge of reaching universal primary education by 2015 becomes even greater. The government of Sierra Leone needs to continue the implementation of free primary education by developing additional strategies to deal with the children who are still not entering the country's education system as opposed to the system of selecting the children of the elites to be educated during the colonial period.

The educational programs are lacking in the elements that

most rapidly foster innovation and economic growth. Even though in the course of time, the curriculum had been broadened, the existing system is too academic and has made a poor showing with regard to the development of the scientific attitude and a critical turn of mind. The system is geared towards literary attainment almost to the utter neglect of training in technical and practical skills. Therefore, the secondary school system is like a one way lane leading to an external examination in academic subjects and this in turn leads either to university entrance or preparation for it.

6.2 Resources

Quality materials including but not limited textbooks, school supplies and technology materials must be made available in a well-structured learning environment in order to achieve superior learning outcomes. Most schools in Sierra Leone have poor classroom conditions and still lack sufficient learning materials. Learning outcomes need to be improved, as evidenced by the BECE, which shows only a 50 percent pass rate in 2010. The inadequacies of such physical infrastructures as school buildings, classroom furniture, and teacher accommodations continue to be major challenges. Therefore, intervention should focus on improvement of overall quality, such as improving teachers' qualifications, reducing class size, increasing accessibility to teaching materials, and better school management.

6.3 Teachers

Another important aspect is the shortage of qualified teachers. The ten year war destroyed the infrastructure of the country's education system and the quality of teaching deteriorated to its lowest. Although the government has doubled enrollment since the war ended, it is very important that the children are provided with access to quality education. The increase in school enrollment has created an acute shortage of qualified teachers and has forced the government to employ unqualified teachers. In 2010, 53% of primary school teachers and 62% of secondary school teachers were unqualified. The rural areas are the hardest hit by the shortage of qualified teachers. Many teachers who graduate from institutions in the capital city and district headquarter towns do not return to their home areas to take employment. As a consequence, rural areas are deprived of qualified teachers. Better deployment and placement procedures are needed to alleviate the acute shortage of qualified teachers in the rural areas. Because teachers can apply directly to their schools of choice and the incentives to work in rural areas are few, the more qualified teachers tend to work in the larger towns.

Although the government, assisted by development partners, is providing in-service training for unqualified teachers, the progress has been slow and the capacity is limited. The negative perception of the teaching profession could be improved by the government paying salaries on time; granting teachers loan facilities; developing a comprehensive and sustainable strategy that comprises pre-service and in-service training; and recruitment, deployment, and retention of motivated, well-paid, and well-resourced professional teachers.

Teachers are essential for delivering education services and improving student learning outcomes. They are crucial to the delivery of a quality education system because they are directly responsible for equipping students with the necessary skills and knowledge. High student-teacher ratio affects the efficiency of the learning environment as it can cause teacher work overload, which in turn may lead to stress, increased absenteeism, and higher attrition rates. Therefore, the management of teachers is important for the effective delivery of education services. More appropriate teacher deployment can help alleviate the high student-teacher ratios especially in the Northern and Eastern regions, where attracting and retaining qualified teachers is particularly challenging. Previously, during the colonial period, schooling was concentrated only in the Western Area and very few areas in other regions, so there was not the problem of high student-teacher ratio or teacher shortage.

6.4 Decentralization

In Sierra Leone, there has been de facto decentralization of teacher management, because recruitment and deployment of personnel was left to the schools themselves due to weak capacity at the central level. When a teacher is hired, the school applies to the Ministry of Education for the teacher to be added to the government payroll. Once the hire is approved by the Ministry of Education, the new employee is added to the payroll. This process can take a long time, resulting in a backlog of teachers to be added to the government payroll.

At present, there are some contradictions between the Education Act and the Local Government Act. Clear lines of authority and accountability have not been drawn. For example, the Education Act (Government of Sierra Leone, 2004, p.8 section 6.3) states that "primary education, and hence all primary schools, shall be controlled and caused to be inspected by the Minister." The same document also says that the local authorities can only set up education committees with the approval of the Minister of Education. However, the Local Government Act states that all functions pertaining to primary education are to be devolved to the local councils. Section 20.3 of the Education Act also states that "the Ministry of Education is to be responsible only for policy making, providing technical guidance to the local councils, and monitoring their performance." The ambiguities in the laws pose a challenge for successful devolution of tasks and responsibilities, therefore the local councils and the Ministry of Education will have to come to a shared understanding of the decentralization strategy, with clear delineation of roles, authority, and functions for the local councils and the Ministry of Education.

One aspect of education innovation in Sierra Leone since the colonial period is the discrepancy between the formulation and implementation of educational policies in the context of the socio-economic and political development process. During the colonial period, the colonial administration formulated policies which were implemented and funded by a separate body - the missionaries. However, educational development and the implementation of education policies have been negatively influenced by a number of factors:

1. Lack of realism of educational policies developed in terms of the availability of resources, skilled manpower for implementation and the social and political characteristics of Sierra Leone.
2. Lack of resources to implement policy. This relates to poor planning at the policy formulation stage where the policymakers set targets based on incorrect calculations or do not take full account of costs involved in the implementation of the policy. The result is that at the implementation phase, the resources are simply not available to implement the policy.
3. Inefficiency, incompetence and inertia of the administrative structure. Decision making is centralized resulting in long delays that negatively affect the efficiency of the education system.
4. Social and cultural factors such as gender, ethnic, religious and socio-economic considerations can create resistance at the implementation stage. It is not uncommon to find rural people resisting certain changes because they do not believe that they are receiving the same treatment as their urban counterparts. The years of war in Sierra Leone not only disrupted the education of children and youth, but left many of them disabled, separated from their families, or orphaned. Today, many young people are illiterate and have no employment skills and little work experience. Unfortunately, despite some noteworthy efforts, the educational policies of the Sierra Leone government did not depart significantly from its

colonial roots. There has been little change in the field of education since independence. Sierra Leone is still struggling to find an uneasy balance between curricula that are culturally relevant and curricula that prepare students to participate effectively in the global village. The rapid expansion of the education system at the primary school level has implications for the quality of education which is related to students' level of achievement and conditions of learning. It places pressure on the secondary school system, prompting questions about how to continue expanding enrollment while also improving the quality of education.

Within the education bureaucracy of post-colonial countries, policymaking generally involves the processing of a collection of ideas and information expressed by experts, scholars, planners, administrators and other officials. In Sierra Leone, as with the other post-colonial countries, policymaking tends to be an extension of practices acquired during the colonial period – a change in the characteristics of the officials, but little change in the framework and process of policymaking. A basic assumption that has guided educational policy development in Africa is that education offers the key to economic growth, restructuring of the social order and reducing the social ills of the country at large (Nieuwenhuis, 1996). However, it would be a fallacy to think that any kind of education would yield the necessary returns. The formulation of education policy can take many forms. The task of translating policies into practice is usually undertaken by curriculum planners, specialists and administrators which can include both nationals and international experts. In Sierra Leone, the current education policy was formulated through commissions on education which reviewed the status quo in education and came up with specific recommendations to guide the policy. The policy formulated was released as a white paper on education. Once the white paper has been adopted by the legislature, it serves as the basis of education policy implementation, a legacy of the colonial administration.

Implementation is not a simple matter of changing existing legislature. It is a combination of technical and administrative processes that must be put in place. It concerns the deployment of resources and expertise. Various factors operating within the administrative structures of government may promote or impede implementation. These include the availability of resources and expertise, the feasibility of the policy, the goodwill of the bureaucrats responsible for implementation and the acceptance of the policy by the larger community (Nieuwenhuis, 1996).

It would be a great mistake, even a dangerous one, to underestimate the influence that colonial education exercised in the period it held sway. It had not only a short term significance, in relation to its immediate objectives, but also because of the long term objectives, it pursued, exercised and continues to exercise a considerable influence on the policies of education in Sierra Leone even today. The overall structure and academic aims of traditional colonial-influenced curricula remain. It should be assumed at this point in the history of the country that education is expected to be geared to the needs of the individual and the nation. Consequently, education must be development-oriented. That being the case, manpower training must, of necessity, be oriented towards the skills needed for the development of the country with openness to new ideas, and an ability to go on learning new skills that the Sierra Leone society demands.

One can easily understand the size of a few of the more obvious problems of present day education in Sierra Leone. They show, for instance, that the ideal of quickly providing some minimum of school education for every child is still far from being realized. The present educational structure is too inflexible to cope with the changing needs of the country in terms of rapid development of the much needed manpower. The educational system is a crisis of maladjustment - of disparities taking many forms - between the system and its social-economic environment. Some of these maladjustments include the gap between educational demand and supply; imbalance between educational output and the economy's manpower needs and misfit between the contents of education, training and the real needs of the society. There is persistent popular demand for more education with unstated purpose. Despite efforts of the educational system to expand (and partly because of this) it has been unable to narrow the gap between the steadily rising popular demand for its service and its capacity to admit more students and give them satisfactory education. This is basically because education breeds its own demand independently of the economy's ability to support it. In addition, the socioeconomic history of Sierra Leone is such that the country has not been able to develop an economic niche and so has not been able to plan for the future skill requirements.

The challenges discussed on the input side of the educational system are also matched by trouble on the output side, taking the form of discrepancies between education, and the employment market. It centers in the structural defects of the economy and the job market; in the rigidities in job classifications and hiring practices, in distorted wage structures, and in the inefficient mechanisms for allocating and utilizing educated manpower. These create a wide distance between the actual demands of the employment market and the amount of educated manpower, which the economy could theoretically use with profit if it were functioning more efficiently. It is therefore imperative to identify the country's human resource development priorities and labor market needs through comprehensive study and consultation.

CHAPTER 7

Planning for the Future in Education

Sierra Leone has a rich educational tradition and occupies a prestigious place in history as having a series of firsts in Western style educational provision in Sub-Saharan Africa: the first secondary school for boys (Sierra Leone Grammar School), founded in 1845; the first secondary school for girls (Annie Walsh Memorial School), founded in 1849; and the first tertiary education institution (Fourah Bay College), founded in 1827.

The right to education is articulated clearly in Article 26 of the United Nations Universal Declaration of Human Rights of 1948. If everyone has the right to education, and if the impact upon people's capabilities is part of our understanding of development, it follows that the provision of a basic level of education for everyone must be universal. 2015 is expected to be the year when all children of the world will be able to get primary education, but there are countries such as Sierra Leone, where it will be very difficult or practically impossible to achieve "Education for All". Despite rapid progress in expanding school enrollment since independence in 1961, many children are still not in school. The quality of education is low, and the education system is dysfunctional. In a country where there is widespread poverty, education for all cannot become a reality without removing barriers to schooling, especially for children from deprived regions or families. However hard the government tries to provide education to all, it still has to cope with the reality that for the mean time, a good number of people will still miss out on this.

Advocates of universal primary education (UPE) believe that mass education will result in an increased supply of educated

Primary and Secondary Education in Sierra Leone

human power, accelerated economic growth, more social justice, reduced regional disparities, and improved social welfare. Wang (2007) indicates that schooling is a dynamic process and a challenging sequence in which children go through several critical phases. Therefore, good governance and management of the education sector is critical for the efficient delivery of education services. The political and social attitudes towards governance and management are changing in Sierra Leone. The local governance reform enacted in 2004 has had significant implications for the education sector because management and control of basic education (primary through junior secondary) have devolved to local government.

Based on these observations, Sierra Leone has to work out new policies in education, not because everything done in the past was wrong but because to proceed along the same lines will not suffice for the future. Sierra Leone is a nation in a hurry, with rapid progress in its political and socio-economic evolution. All this will founder, unless and until progress in its educational thinking and practice develop side by side with progress in other fields. With Sierra Leone in the middle of rehabilitation and reconstruction, recent trends indicate that the bottleneck in manpower is the availability of a pool of skilled workers of high quality and functional adequacy in different occupational specifications. If in future an entrepreneur builds a factory designed to manufacture the simplest product involving the use of standard machine tools and production operations, there is no guarantee that he/she can go out into the labor market and recruit the operators and craftsmen he needs to start with. This is because little emphasis has been placed on vocational and technical education for the middle-level manpower.

One of the first needs of the vast majority of individuals is to be rendered capable of meeting the needs of society and finding a satisfactory life within it, a society that is development conscious and working actively to become developed. Therefore, if Sierra Leone is to come closer to the achievement of such a society, its educational system has to be oriented in content and method towards a number of individual and collective ends. It must provide for the individual opportunity for acquiring basic skills and knowledge that can be applied to the solution of the problems of everyday life. This therefore calls for a change of direction from quantitative to qualitative educational growth because to continue enlarging the existing system of education which has evolved from the earlier concept of general educational growth in the sectors of education is a recipe for educational and economic confusion.

In Sierra Leone, people acquire education to earn a good enough income and be able to continue the family life. This seems to be the strongest motivational force pushing many Sierra Leoneans to go to great lengths in giving their children good education. Education must enable the members of its society to live a happier, fuller and more constructive life. To play a satisfying part in society, one must understand and to some extent accept the nature of the society in which one is living and the purpose of the work which one does. In this case, Sierra Leone's educational purpose has to be in line with the national purpose; to create a good society and a good life for all the members and to use all the intellectual and moral resources it has developed and the resources it is capable of developing, in the pursuit of this goal.

Education in any society is a great boon, but it can also be a great curse if all it succeeds in doing is to stratify it by creating people who are conscious only of what society owes to them and not what they owe the society in which they have been brought up. If Sierra Leone's education program is to have any meaning for life, it must pass through a transformation. Therefore, in formulating new policies of education for the Sierra Leone society, policy makers have to be largely concerned with changes which could make it more relevant to the kind of society they live in. They have to be concerned with what the future of education ought to be and with what it probably will be. This means that the education system of a country cannot be properly judged in a vacuum, but in the light of the goals.

What is now urgently needed is a realistic reappraisal of present educational policies in relation to its relevance to social and economic development; restructuring the system in such a way as to provide educational opportunities to match the characteristics and needs of the society. Education should provide a countervailing force, in the sense that it should widen the capacity of the individual for participation, for personal judgment, for choice and for enjoyment, by making learners aware of the changing ways of their own environment and their underlying causes as well as, of the best that has been thought and said in the past. Only to the extent that the student is educated in this way, to the limits of his or her own powers, can the learner make himself/herself as an individual, as fully responsible as any of us can be for his/her own life. Preparation of a revised education plan will therefore be a good opportunity for the government to review the current policies and practices and learn lessons from the past years to shed light on how to move forward more rapidly.

A current major challenge confronting the governing class is how to develop an effective educational system that can meet the national aspirations and the demands of the people. From time to time, national needs make the nation as a whole sit up to think about the direction of education. Sierra Leoneans must, in the first place, decide why they educate at all, what contribution they expect people to make to society as a result of education. It may be suggested that Sierra Leoneans now face the task of seeking out alternatives and of building up an educational system which may be better able to meet the diversity of their needs through employing a diversity of means. If education is the aggregate of all the processes by means of which a person develops abilities, attitudes and other forms of behavior of positive value in the society in which he/she lives; if it is a system based on certain philosophical or theoretical assumptions seeking to justify its usefulness in terms of its practices and results, then the educational system in Sierra Leone can hardly stand the test. This is a period when clichés and superficial recipes can no longer solve their problems, however temporarily. Effective education then, strikes a harmonious balance between the needs of the society. It has to bring the individual to a point where he/she can do a job of work with such skill, intelligence, taste and responsibility that his/her occupation becomes a source of creative and satisfying living. The education programs in Sierra Leone, therefore, have to be interrelated in order to fulfill this role.

However, viewed in historical perspective rather than from the easy wisdom generated by hindsight, the evolution of the attitude towards the social function of education was inevitable and not wholly to be regretted. The formal education provided in schools constituted a foundation for the spread of literacy and higher education, and it also made possible the increasing expansion of education in all sectors. But to continue this old pattern of education in the 21st century would spell disaster. The time for change is long overdue, for the past decades have been largely wasted. You cannot use yesterday's tools for today's job and expect to be in business tomorrow. The problem it appears, is how to reform the education system, to make it more relevant to root them more completely in the culture of the society and to produce an educational system capable of preparing young people for their modernizing role without divorcing them from their culture, because an inappropriate education or an education inappropriately applied may be worse than useless.

Sierra Leone has weak human capacity at all levels of the public service, a situation brought on by many years of corrupt governance exacerbated by ten years of civil war which makes this issue one of the most critical challenges facing Sierra Leone today. A transformation in public sector pay and incentive structures may be necessary, along with an aggressive capacity building agenda. Currently, the capacity in managing human, financial, and physical resources for the education sector is weak in most local councils. Nieuwenhuis (1996) noted that education is a subsystem within the larger state and political dispensation, which includes the government of the day. He further indicated that such a government will, preferably in consultation with its constituency, take decisions concerning education based on its own political agenda as well as certain historical, socio-cultural, religious and economic factors.

Sierra Leone is moving toward decentralization. The decentralization process has good potential for success, but some issues need to be addressed to achieve a smooth implementation. Local capacity is among many factors that play a key role in determining whether decentralization will lead to better education service delivery. Glewwe & Kremer (2005) indicated that local communities have the best knowledge about the needs of their children, and strong incentives to monitor the performance of teachers and school administrators. Local councils and the Ministry of Education therefore need to work together to develop a capacity building plan to ensure that the developed functions can be effectively managed and that schools and children truly benefit from decentralization.

Local councils will be held accountable for government and government-assisted primary and junior secondary schools. Their responsibilities will include payment of teachers and student fees, provision of teaching materials, rehabilitation of schools, and inspection of teachers and students. It is therefore important for the central government to help strengthen the capacity at the local level and make local councils accountable for delivering education services and diligently supervising schools, so that the learning environment and learning outcomes can in turn be improved.

The country's education system is recovering from the debilitating destruction of war and in years to come, will continue to deal with problems caused by the war. Priorities will shift from implementing emergency programs for reestablishing basic service delivery to designing and achieving fiscally sustainable long-term development for the education sector. Ten years after the war, the education system has achieved an extraordinary recovery, reflected in the massive increase of student enrollments. The education system has great potential for sustainable development but major challenges remain.

One of the problems of educational planning in Sierra Leone is that of accurately forecasting national requirements. The rate of change is so rapid that projections are out of date before they are implemented. No single educational pattern will retain forever its relevance and efficiency in rapidly changing societies. Innumerable factors may alter original projections. This emphasizes the importance of flexibility in planning which must always take account of factors such as human element, social change, and political and economic pressures.

The government is committed to implementing nine years of universal basic education, but given the enormous financial outlay and immense capacity required to enroll all children in junior secondary school and then ensure they can complete it, a realistic and sustainable plan must be developed. Whatever Sierra Leone's level of development, there is great demand for education reform in order to be able to face political, social, and cultural changes, as well as scientific and technological transformation. This reform represents human and financial challenges. As such, detailed strategies are required to ensure that schools receive the financial and administrative support they require to provide the basic educational services.

These suggested reforms can improve the educational practices in Sierra Leone

1. Teachers have a critical and unique role to play in the provision of quality schooling. The teacher questionnaire shows that there is a serious teacher morale issue in the country. An improvement in policies for hiring, training, housing, and paying teachers should be a priority.
2. There is also an urgent need in the education sector to establish a management information system that will allow the Ministry of Education to have complete and reliable information to plan, monitor, and evaluate

performance. This system can be used to conduct high quality school census to capture relevant data, and a student learning assessment program.
3. Financial resources play a key role in delivering quality education services. To mobilize more domestic funds and attract more international resources for education from the primary level upward, Sierra Leone needs to show clear evidence of the effective use of funds already available, together with a credible plan for utilizing future additional resources. It also needs to inform and influence international donors on all critical areas of policy improvement in education.

The impetus for this had been to understand the educational problem in Sierra Leone and to respond to those challenges. Research studies can provide the information needed by government to make informed decisions on future directions in education. Education should help us discover who we are and what we are capable of doing to improve human relationships, living conditions and to be stewards of our environment. It is a powerful force for creating the right information, shaping attitudes, and developing the moral and intellectual fiber of a society. It is in this light that this book was published and hopes it may serve as input to the debate on future education policy development in Sierra Leone.

Education is widely regarded as "the route to economic prosperity, the key to scientific and technological advancement, the means to combat unemployment, the foundation of social equity, and the spread of political socialization and cultural vitality" (Chimombo, 2005). While many lessons may have been learnt from the experiences from 50 years of Independence in Sierra Leone, there is need for increased number of studies that should shape educational policies. Suggested areas of future research in education should include but not limited to finance and expenditure, disparity in schooling, gender and equity, school administrators training, special curricula for Post Trauma Student

Disorder, and influence of international funding agencies on policy making.

REFERENCES

Anderson, C. & Foster, P. (1970). *Africa in the Seventies and Eighties: Issues in Development.* New York, Praeger Publishers.

Arianayagam, K. (1970). Prospects in Education. *UNESCO,* 30(2).

Ayandele, E. A. (1971). The Coming of Western Education to Africa. *West African Journal of Education,* 15(1).

Banya, K. (1991). Economic Decline and the Education System: The Case of Sierra Leone. *Comparative Education,* 21(2).

Bethke, L. (2004). *Analysis of Educational Opportunities for Refugee and Displaced Children and Adolescents.* Ph.D. Dissertation. University of Wisconsin-Madison.

Bogdan, R. C. & Biklen, S. K. (2006). *Qualitative Research in Education: An Introduction to Theory and Methods.* (5th Ed.). Pearson Education, Inc.

Brown, G. & Hiskett, M. (1975). *Conflict and Harmony in Education in Tropical Africa.* London, Allen and Unwin.

Buck, R. E. (1975). *A Model for the Development of an African Literature Curriculum in the Secondary Schools of Sierra Leone.* Ph.D. Dissertation. University of North Carolina at Greensboro.

Childs, H. A. (1949). *Plan of Economic Development for Sierra Leone.* Freetown, Government Printers.

Chimombo, J. P. (2005). Issues in Basic Education in Developing Countries: An Exploration of Policy Options for Improved Delivery. *Journal of International Cooperation in Education,* 8(1).

Coleson, E. P. (1956). *Educational Change in Sierra Leone*. Ph.D. Dissertation, University of Michigan.

Datta, A. (1984). *A Sociology of African Education*. London, Macmillan.

Fafunwa, A. B. (1963). African Education and Social Dynamics. *West African Journal of Education*, 7(2).

Fafunwa, A. B. & Aisiku, J. U. (1982). *Education in Africa*. London, Allen and Unwin.

Fajana, A. (1970). Missionary Educational Policy in Nigeria: 1842-1888. *West African Journal of Education*, 14(2).

Fyle, D. (1986). *History of Sierra Leone*. London, Oxford Press.

Glewwe, P. & Kremer, M. (2005). *Schools, Teachers, and Education in Developing Countries*. Handbook on the Economics of Education.

Johnson, B. & Christensen, L. (2004). *Educational Research: Quantitative, Qualitative, and Mixed Approaches*. Pearson Education, Inc.

Kallon, M. (1996). *An Interpretive Study of Planned Educational Reform in Sierra Leone: The Primary School and Teacher Education*. Ph.D. Dissertation. University of Toronto, Canada.

Kandel, I. L. (1961). Comparative Education and Underdeveloped Countries: A New Dimension. *Comparative Education Review*, 4(3).

Kanu, Y. (2007). Tradition and Educational Reconstruction in Africa in Postcolonial and Global Times: *The Case for Sierra Leone*.

African Studies Quarterly – *The Online Journal of African Studies*, 9(3).

Levy, B. & Kpundeh, S. (2004). *Building State Capacity in Africa: New Approaches, Emerging Lessons.* World Bank, Washington, DC.

Lebby, S. J. (1980). *The Development of Elementary Education Policy and Practice in Sierra Leone, 1924–1976.* D.Ed. Dissertation. Pennsylvania State University, Pennsylvania.

Makulu, H. F. (1971). *Education, Development and Nation Building in Independent Africa.* London.

Mayhew, A. (1938). *Education in Colonial Empire.* London, Longmans, Green and Company.

McIver, S. (2006). Interpretive Theory in the Analysis of Citizenship Policy. *Workshop, University of Edinburgh, Scotland.*

McMillan, J. & Schumacher, S. (1997). *Research in Education.* Addison-Wesley Educational Publishers Inc.

Mottier, V. (2005). The Interpretive Turn: History, Memory, and Storage in Qualitative. Research. *Qualitative Social Research*, 6(2).

Moumouni, A. (1968). *Education in Africa.* London, Deutsch.

Nieuwenhuis, F. J. (1996). *The Development of Education Systems in Postcolonial Africa: A Study of a Selected Number of African Countries.* South Africa, Human Sciences Research Council.

Nicol, F. (1991). *The Secondary School Curriculum and its Relevance to the Manpower Needs of Sierra Leone.* Ph.D. Dissertation. University of Maryland, Maryland.

Nyerere, J. (1967). *Education for Self Reliance.* Dar es Salaam, Government Printer.

Peterson, J. (1969). Province of freedom: *A History of Sierra Leone.* London, Faber & Faber.

Phenix, P. H. (1961). Education and the Common Good: A Moral Philosophy of the Curriculum. *http://religion-online.org*

Radnor, H (2002). *Researching Your Professional Practice: Doing interpretive research.* Open University Press.

Resnick, I. N. (1968). *Tanzania: Revolution by Education.* Longmans of Tanzania.

Rotimi, B. O. (1960). Education: Early European Attempts in West Africa. *West African Journal of Education,* 4(3).

Sengova, T. (1982). *Curriculum Policies and Classroom Practices: An Illuminative Study of Sierra Leone Primary Curriculum.* Ph.D. Dissertation. University of Wisconsin, Madison.

Sierra Leone, (1924). *Annual Report of the Board of Education of Sierra Leone.* Freetown, Government Printers.

Sierra Leone Government. (1962). *Ten Year Plan of Economic and Social Development for Sierra Leone, 1962/63-1971/72* Freetown, Government Printers.

Sierra Leone Government. (1970). *The White Paper on Education: Policy.* Freetown, Government Printers.

Sierra Leone Government. (1974). *National Development Plan 1974/75 - 78/79.* Freetown, Government Printers.

Sierra Leone Government. (1976). *The Sierra Leone Education Review.* Freetown, Government Printers.

Sierra Leone Government. (1995). *New Educational Policy For Sierra Leone*. Freetown, Government Printers.

Sierra Leone Government. (2004). *The Education Act, 2004*. Freetown, Government Printers.

Sierra Leone Government. (2006). *Population Census*. Central Statistics Office.

Sierra Leone, Ministry of Youth, Education and Sport (2001). Status of Education in Sierra Leone. *Report of the Rapid School Survey*.

Smart, N. D.. J. (1993). The 6-3-3-4 System of Education and its Implication. *Conference Paper*, Freetown, Sierra Leone.

Sommer, R. & Sommer, B. (2002). A Practical Guide to Behavioral Research: Tools and Techniques. Oxford University Press.

Sumner, D. L. (1964). *Education of Sierra Leone*. Norwich, Jarrold and Sons, Ltd.

Timity, R. J. (1983). *A Needs Assessment of Sierra Leone's Educational System in the 20th Century*. Ph.D. Dissertation. Washington, D. C., Catholic University of America.

Walker, A. (1963). *Official Publications of Sierra Leone and Gambia*, Washington, D. C., Library of Congress.

Wang, L. (2007). *Education in Sierra Leone: Present Challenges, Future Opportunities*. The World Bank, Washington, D.C.

Watson, K. (1994). Technical and Vocational Education in Developing Countries: Western Paradigms and Comparative Methodology. *Comparative Education*, 30(2)

Wilson, J. (1963). *Education and Changing West African Culture*. New York, Columbia University.

Wood, A. W. (1974). *Informal Education and Development in Africa*. New York, Publications of the Institute of Social Studies.

Wurie, A. (2003). Closing the Gap: Access, Inclusion, Achievements. *A paper delivered by Sierra Leone's Minister of Education at the 2003 National Symposium on Education in Sierra Leone*.

www.ingramcontent.com/pod-product-compliance
Lightning Source LLC
Chambersburg PA
CBHW061451040426
42450CB00007B/1315